Praise for Joh̲...

Memoirs of a Mug Punter

'It's impossible not to share Harms' enthusiasm for the horse, and impossible not to take a liking to the writer. There's a gentle and intelligent self mockery in *Memoirs of a Mug Punter* that takes it out of the realm of the self-indulgent, and into the realm of the truly enjoyable.'
Australian Bookseller and Publisher

'Harms is a keen observer of Australian social quirks and rituals.' *West Australian*

'Light of touch, unsentimental, shrewdly paced.'
Canberra Times

'Anyone who is into sport or likes a good laugh will enjoy this book.' *Brisbane News*

'A light entertaining read for those who love a punt just a bit too much.' *Sunday Age*

Confessions of a Thirteenth Man

'Alternating between the funny, the profound and the genuinely touching, Harms has written a book that has been needed in Australia for some time.' *Who Weekly*

'An entertaining and perceptive cultural portrait.'
Australian

'A sheer pleasure to read.' *Courier-Mail*

'Extends the boundaries of Australian sports writing.'
Cricket Lore

John Harms is a freelance writer. He lives in Brisbane. This is his third book.

LOOSE MEN EVERYWHERE

JOHN HARMS

Text Publishing Melbourne Australia

The Text Publishing Company
171 La Trobe Street
Melbourne Victoria 3000
Australia

First published by The Text Publishing Company 2002
Design by Chong Weng-ho
Typeset by J&M Typesetters
Printed and bound by Griffin Press

National Library of Australia
Cataloguing-in-Publication data:
    Harms, John, 1962–.
    Loose men everywhere.

    ISBN 1 876485 88 4.

    1. Football fans - Australia - Humor. 2. Australian
    football - Humor. I. Title.

796.336

For the Harms family—and anyone else who knows
what it means to love the Geelong Football Club.

'There are loose men everywhere.'
Tim Lane, any given Saturday

PART 1

Now faith is the assurance of things hoped for, the
conviction of things unseen.

Hebrews 11:1

CHAPTER I

You have to be born somewhere.

I could have been born into some comfortable blue-stone villa in Hawthorn, just up the road from Glenferrie Oval, in which case the whole of the 1970s and 1980s would have been a far more pleasant experience. I'd have been given a middle name like Poutney. I'd have had a floppy college-boy haircut, made smokes-money out of trading footy cards and skipped to the music of half a dozen great Hawk premierships. I would have been a happy and optimistic child. I would have liked Leigh Matthews. I would have been sent off to some school held together by the twin virtues of Gilbert and Sullivan where I'd have wagged cadets, preferring the company of my mate's sister up the back of the rowing shed. And today I would be a happy and optimistic adult; a Gillette-ad husband and father who believes in his own goodness and honesty and consequently, after a few glasses of Hill of Grace, is forced to make hot-eared admissions that he likes things like John Howard's power walk and Channel 9 cricket memorabilia. I'd own shares and BMWs in a ratio of about fifty-five to one. I'd sleep easily at night knowing that in every Hawthorn person like me there is some John Kennedy and Chris Mew and Chris Langford: the sort of men who hold the world together.

Or I could have been born into a housing commission fibro in Footscray, in which case the 1970s and 1980s would have been a far more pleasant experience because I wouldn't have had to go to school, or felt pressured to achieve anything. I'd have just lived—and lived proudly—west of the Maribyrnong. And I wouldn't have expected Footscray to win a premiership, so just following the footy would have been enough. I'd have had a short and long haircut (part in the middle) that Dougie Hawkins would have died for, and traded in left hooks and durries. I'd have made money selling *Footy Record*s on the Geelong Road end of the Western Oval to save up for me first tattoo—Elmer Fudd pointing a shotgun at me freckle and saying, 'Come out you wascally wabbit.' And when the hormones kicked in I would have got meself a Sandman and an Angels album and set about repopulating Sunshine off me own bat. These days I'd be a happy adult who loves pizza and Homer Simpson and the serenity at Lake Eildon. I'd still have me Dennis Lillee moustache and I'd have only cried a couple of times in me life: once when Teddy did the lap at the MCG and the other time when Chris Grant didn't go to Port Adelaide.

At least if I'd been born in Hawthorn or Footscray I'd have some idea of who I was.

I wasn't. I was born in a little town cut out of the brigalow scrub on the rich black soil of the western Darling Downs. The town of Chinchilla would have been fine if I'd been born into a Catholic rugby league family, or was the son of some sun-spotted rugger-loving grazier who'd been to school at Churchie in Brisbane. Things might have made sense then. But I was born into a life of confusion and frustration, a life of upset and despondency, a life of tears.

I was born a Geelong supporter.

Not only was I born a Geelong supporter but I was born in exile; a Geelong supporter in the Queensland bush, where people had no idea of what footy was or meant. I suspect I hit the light of day, felt the blue and white pulsing through my veins, looked out the window and immediately frowned, 'There must be a mistake. Are you sure? Is this right?'

I was born in round nine of the 1962 VFL season. Geelong lost only four games in the entire home and away season that year, but I was born in the week of one of them: a forty-point flogging at Windy Hill. It was a season so quintessentially Geelong that it has led me to believe the Jesuits got it wrong with the seven years business. Their dictum should be: 'Give me the boy for the last nine rounds of his first footy season and I will show you the man.' We finished second on the ladder, behind the Bombers, and then in the second semi-final we led them at half time but faded in the second half (stopped to a walk actually). We then played a valiant draw with Carlton in the preliminary final, but the following week we lost the replay by five points. Essendon went on to beat Carlton in the grand final.

They are now the two most successful clubs in the league.

That summer I was put on the back seat of the EK Holden and taken south to live in Wangaratta in north-eastern Victoria. I took quite a shine to Wangaratta, most likely because in the first year we were there Geelong won the flag. I am very pleased that Geelong won the flag in 1963 because if we hadn't we wouldn't have won a premiership in half a century. But it's just so typical of being a Geelong supporter: I was too young to remember our only triumph.

In Wangaratta we became a family. Two brothers, Peter and David, arrived. We had a little brick house with sweet peas and a sandpit and a cat called Thomas. Next door was the steep-roofed Lutheran church where my father was the minister.

Being a minister wasn't a job for my father. It was a

calling; a vocation; a life. He was deeply, proudly and confidently Lutheran. He was also a father. And he was a Geelong supporter. These things were in his heart. His father—Papa—was a Lutheran minister. My great-grandfather was also a Lutheran minister. We were a Lutheran family. But we were also a Geelong family. My great-grandfather and Papa loved Geelong. My uncle loved Geelong. My cousins loved Geelong. When we got together there was always plenty of chat about the mighty Cats. At Christmas time it was, 'Hark the herald angels sing. Glory to the new born king. Amen. How do you think Polly Farmer will go as coach?'

Dad grew up with footy. He was six when Geelong won the flag in 1937. He was a student in Adelaide during the Cats' glorious years of 1951–52. Dad saw the VFL semi-final in 1952 when Geelong thrashed Collingwood. At the seminary there were two great faiths: Lutheranism and football. Some of his seminary mates played footy for Sturt and West Adelaide.

My mother was a farm girl from the Lockyer Valley. Her father—Grandpa Logan—grew potatoes and pumpkins and watermelons. He ate boiled peanuts and bought tickets in the Golden Casket. He had been a sprinter and a rugby league winger and he wore one of those woollen undershirts that players used to wear in the old days. My mother met my father at Luther League, one of those hormone-corralling church youth organisations. When it came to footy and Geelong my mother didn't know what the fuss was all about.

Wangaratta became home. We played. Mum read us stories. Dad told us stories. We went to church. We were very happy. We went for drives. Dad would buy two bob's worth of hot chips which would steam themselves in butcher's paper while he drove us down to the railway line. We'd sit in the warm car and share the soggy chips while we waited for the Spirit of Progress to go past. We loved the little salty, crispy chips at the end. There were never enough. We also loved trains.

At this time I can only assume that there was footy in our household—because there has always been footy in our household. We didn't have a television and I can't remember Dad listening to footy on the radio but somehow, along the way, footy's omnipresence must have had its effect. I can remember a time when I wasn't interested in golf or girls, but I can't remember a time without footy. I can't remember a time when I didn't think of footy with a satisfied fondness.

My first specific recollection of the VFL comes from the mid-sixties when Dad took me to Moorabbin to watch Geelong play St Kilda. I have a few fossilised bone-fragments of memory from which I have constructed a whole beast. It is an overcast day; showery. I am a little scared as we walk along. I am drifting in a current of legs. Dad holds my hand and directs me. Sometimes he lifts me and my feet come off the ground. He is wearing his gaberdine overcoat, the sort that Norm Smith or Ben Chifley used to wear. During the game I stand on a wooden form along the fence, but when I still can't see, Dad puts me on his shoulders. Water splashes on my head. Dad tries to keep me dry by holding his newspaper above me. No one behind him complains. I can remember figures out on the ground—footballers. There is noise. I can't remember who wins. My strongest memory is of the grey streaks of ink which have trickled down my face, and of the dull, dull light. When, twenty years later, I see Arthur Streeton's *National Game* for the first time, I am reminded of that day at Moorabbin.

My brothers and I loved to play. We *vroom*ed matchbox cars along the roads we had built. We were cowboys and Indians. We were drivers of long trains made of cardboard cartons. We ran. We chased each other. We played with anything which could be kicked and thrown and punched and caught. Mum preferred that that didn't include each other.

Inside the house we played balloon-footy. Balloons were objects of mystery: they went from something to nothing very quickly and with a force that scared you and why couldn't kids blow them up? Why did they smell? Why did they break if you took them outside?

They were also objects of fun. You would always run at the balloon on the floor with earnest focus and absolute determination. Sometimes you'd swing your tiny leg at the balloon with the timing of Dave MacNamara and it would fly towards the ceiling and you'd laugh and bring your hands together in a single clap and look at your mother for approval and then you'd run after it and compete with your brothers to catch it on the way down. Other times your foot would almost miss and you'd plonk down on your bottom (which was what it was called in those days) and the frustration would consume you. You always wanted to kick it further—but you couldn't. And when you did connect properly you'd jump three or four times at the balloon while it hung in the air. You'd reach desperately, seeking possession of it. And then, when you were just about to catch it, your Vegemite fingernails would cause an almighty bang and you'd get a huge fright and run off to your bedroom fighting off tears of disappointment, and tears of fear because you didn't know; you didn't understand balloons. And your father would come in and humour you. He'd pull tight on a piece of the broken balloon rubber and suck up an air bubble and twist and twist until it made his eyes go funny and his cheeks cave in. And the bubble would get really, really tight and your mother would hand you a pin and your dad would hold the little bubble in front of you and say, 'Go on,' and you wouldn't have the courage to prick the bubble and you'd look at your mother to see if it was OK and she'd look at you with eyes that made you know that it was. You'd clench your teeth and try for their sake if not for your own but you couldn't do it, and Dad would never show any frustration that you couldn't do it, because he loved you, and then he'd push the bubble to where you were holding the pin and there'd be a high-pitched pop and you'd look at both of them as if to say, 'I did it,' and you were actually still a bit funny about it.

But you wanted another balloon blown up so you could kick it.

Outside the house we kicked the brown plastic footy. We advanced from the kick off the ground to the real kick (like the footy players on telly) passing through the standard evolutionary stages. First attempts at this proper kick began with the ball in both hands out in front and a look of serious concentration. The motion was initiated by tossing the plastic footy into the air, like a tennis serve, at which point the brain would send a message to the foot to strike at the appropriate instant. But the foot was slow to receive the message. The toss was often so wayward that the designated kicking foot might have needed to handle an urgent intermediate signal from the brain, that being to assist its partner foot in running to the position where the ball was falling, such that the foot might make contact with the ball. (Sometimes there would be a late decision to kick with the undesignated foot.) This intermediate step was gradually phased out and we were able to stand in the one position to kick the footy. Usually some contact was made. Sometimes it grubbered along the ground. Sometimes it went back over our heads. But we could do it—well enough to keep us happy. And it was fun. The plastic footy was so hard at each of its end points, though, that kicks which could be recognised as part of the drop punt species would break your foot and you'd hop around saying, 'That killed. That killed!' Most kids have at some stage been disheartened by the plastic footy. It is one of life's impediments.

In 1967 Dad accepted a 'call' and we moved up the road to the fruit town of Shepparton. He became pastor in what the Lutheran church called a 'mission field'. His congregation consisted of Australian Lutherans and displaced Europeans. The 'new Australians' were different. They looked different. The men wore their hair like Romulus Gaita; the women wore scarves rather than hats. When we visited them they served weird food which they explained to us proudly. They were poor but generous. Sometimes they laughed. But I could sense their sadness. Once I sang 'Silent Night' in German for Mr and Mrs Muecke. The tears ran down their cheeks. I still remember it:

Stille Nacht heilige Nacht
Alles schläft einsam Wacht
Schlaf in himmelische Ruh
Schlaf in himmelische Ruh

There were a few Germans, Latvians and Estonians. Guntus Gelevics who was younger than me used to chant Dad's bits of the liturgy. This made us feel uneasy, because that wasn't how things were supposed to happen.

We knew how things were supposed to happen. Lutherans knew the truth.

The truth wasn't all that difficult in those days. God was all-powerful and all-knowing. Some days He was a God of wrath but, gladly and happily, in our home He was a loving God. Kind. Generous. And, significantly, forgiving. He was always with us. The plaque on the kitchen wall reminded us that:

Christ is the head of this house
The unseen guest at every meal
The silent listener to every conversation

We said grace: 'Come, Lord Jesus, be our guest, and let this food to us be blessed. Amen.' We were thankful that we had food. We were sad for the starving children in Africa and China. We prayed that they would be baptised before they died. We worried about the natives overseas. An uncle was a missionary in New Guinea and an aunt was the matron of a hospital on Kar Kar Island. We did our bit too. We saved stamps for missions and we collected five-cent pieces in special mission containers. I hardly thought of the Aborigines although I knew that Albert Namatjira was a good painter from our mission at Hermannsburg.

I went to sleep safe and secure in the knowledge of my own Baptism. God loved me and cared for me. I was comforted by my mother's voice as she said our prayers:

Now I lay me down to sleep
I pray Thee Lord my soul to keep
If I should die before I wake
I pray Thee Lord my soul to take
Amen

I wasn't scared of dying because I was a child of God and I was going to Heaven. My mother tucked me in and reassured me, 'Dying is just like going to sleep.'

On Sunday mornings we would all get dressed up and walk across the yard and into the church where Dad would take the service. We would flick through books and play with the plastic animals and swing our legs and listen to the organ and hum the hymns and it would take a long time and then we'd run around outside.

At home we had a Bible reading each night and we sang:

Jesus loves me, this I know
For the Bible tells me so
Little ones to Him belong
They are weak but He is strong

We knew. We didn't believe: we knew. And we belonged. We always belonged.

CHAPTER 2

It's probably a good thing that I can't remember Geelong losing the 1967 grand final. My first memory of barracking for the Cats comes from the end of the 1968 season. It is a sunny spring day. Dad is in the front yard of our new house preparing the ground to sow a lawn. He has already planted a few saplings: a liquidambar, a claret ash and a blue spruce. He is wearing shorts. His legs are white. He has a white floppy hat on; one of those ones with a green lining. His wireless sits in its brown leather case. It is tuned, as always, to the ABC. Geelong is playing Essendon in the preliminary final as Dad spreads a layer of sand across the turned soil. I watch him while sitting next to the footy. It's a proper leather footy. I have been sitting on it but have been told to get off as a footy is not for sitting on. I am waiting for Dad to finish so we can have a kick, yet I am too young to know one of the great axioms of the Australian backyard: work in the garden or the shed will be carried out at a pace which has the job finished at the time of the final siren.

I stand up and kick the footy to myself, and punch one end to make it spin around in my left hand. I know not to stray onto the sandy area. Dad keeps working. He half whistles: a sort of blow-whistle which indicates that there is other work in progress as well. It usually means he is thinking about Sunday's sermon, only today he is concentrating on the footy. He can't be distracted. It's close. Geelong loses.

I am too young to notice his disappointment.

The following year I was very excited when I realised footy season was about to start. Dad and Mum sat me down and told me that I was at a stage in my life when I should keep a football scrapbook. I bought a 64-page Embassy mapping book which would become my season's archive. Each Tuesday I cut out the 'VFL Details' from Monday's Melbourne *Sun*. We had a rule in our house that the paper had to be at least a day old before it could in any way be violated. I would also cut out photographs which featured Geelong players. I was so thrilled when there was a Geelong photograph in the paper. Then I would get the Clag and, having considered an appropriate layout, would put the round's summary together. The role of Clag in football should never be underestimated.

We waited for the start of that season—and then had to wait two more days because in 1969 Geelong's opening match was on Easter Monday. Dad was almost always busy but on this Easter Monday, with his Easter schedule out of the way, he was free. He decided to take us all fishing.

We are all very pleased about this prospect and pile into the Morris 1100 (which floats on fluid) and drive to one of the irrigation channels in the countryside. It is an eastern bloc waterway where function triumphs over beauty. It is far from idyllic. We look like that family in the Leunig cartoon where they are having a picnic in an inner-city car park. All it needs is for someone to say, 'Gee Dad, you're fantastic!' The Morris 1100 is parked by the water's edge and we prepare to fish. We have hand reels rather than rods. The principal considera-tion is the placement of Dad's wireless. We are excited. The broadcast match is Geelong–Melbourne. It's hardly ever Geelong on the ABC. We have never been fishing before. Dad and Mum explain what a nibble is. They tell us what to do. They are pestered to bait hooks. Dad listens to the footy. So do I. In fact I listen to it more than he does. David shows all the initiative expected from a four-year-old and heads up the channel. His worm looks like it's been dragged through the dirt (because it has) and he drops it into the channel. He yells out that he has a nibble. He's a fast learner. I yell out that Ken Newland has kicked a goal and that the Stawell Gift is about to be on. Mum yells that he should pull it in. I yell out that we're still ten points behind. David walks backwards to pull his hook from the water. Then he screams. I ask Dad if he thinks we can win. A yabby walks up the bank towards David and, like an overweight full forward, David doesn't know how to change direction. He is petrified. Mum rescues him. We catch some fish. David regains his composure.

Geelong fights back in the second half. David is looking down the steep bank when he topples forward. Dad grabs his gumboot which looks like it will come off in his hand. He adjusts the angle and it is enough to keep David from falling in. Dad and Mum are more relieved than they show. Geelong wins. I am more relieved than anyone. We go home. That night we eat redfin and homemade chips. We watch the footy replay.

I loved Geelong so much that Mum and Dad gave me a Geelong jumper for my birthday—one of those old woollen ones with a collar and no patch on the back for a number. I had to wear a T-shirt under it because it was so scratchy. I wanted a number—number 35—but I knew to be thankful for what I had. I also had woollen Geelong socks.

By grade two standards, my scrapbook was kept meticulously that season. There were plenty of Geelong victories to Clag in, and each week I'd create a couple of pages of historical record. The photos and articles are surprisingly ecumenical: they are not just about Geelong. '300th League Game Big Kick For Ted Whitten', 'Star Solo Act: Billy Goggin', 'Hudson's in the 100's...again', 'Closterphobia'.

In the week Neil Armstrong walked on the moon I was more interested in Geelong's win against Footscray. It looked like we were going to make the four. We were a chance of winning the flag. Billy Goggin and Ian Nankervis just kept hitting Doug Wade on the chest and he just kept splitting the middle with those huge punt kicks. He kicked 127 goals that year. I loved him. I loved them all.

They were my heroes. Not my first heroes, though—I knew great men from the Bible stories Mum and Dad read to us. I knew what they looked like because we had a book of Bible stories with grand, painted pictures. They were brave like David who killed Goliath and like Daniel in the lions' den. They were great leaders like Moses who trusted God and believed he could do miraculous things. And, of course, Jesus. Why did he have to suffer on the cross? He was very brave.

Footballers were also brave and they did miraculous things as well—especially Geelong footballers. We did make the four that year, which was a great thrill, but it was during the finals that I was alerted to the existence of my soul and introduced to the injury the Geelong Football Club can inflict upon it. You must be forever vigilant where your soul is concerned if you barrack for Geelong otherwise you can lose your faith in life itself.

We waited all week for the first semi. We knew it was a special week because on Friday morning the paper included the age, heights and weights of each of the players. Please win. Please win. We weren't a household who prayed for Geelong. We prayed for a good, fair game, and that the best team would win. Secretly I hoped for some outside assistance.

I offered my own help. I gave myself little tests. 'If I can put this drop kick between the peach and the apricot trees Geelong will win on Saturday.' Dad didn't like it when my kick hit the post and his blossoms went flying. 'If I can hold my breath for a minute Geelong will win on Saturday.' I sat with my chest caved in and my temples bursting and then I'd splutter and gasp as I recovered. 'If I can throw a twenty, the Cats are home.' The ancient plastic darts didn't fly too well.

We waited. We listened. Geelong played very, very badly. They lost to Richmond by 118 points. I couldn't believe it. No team lost by 118 points. Why Geelong? I had been disappointed before but this was something new; something more. It was this sad feeling; a sort of emptiness. There were no tears; just a sigh and the need to reach for your mother's comfort; a hope that she would come and sit with you and stroke your forehead.

Dad always knew what to say. 'We'll try again next year; we'll come back.' He always said stuff like that. He knew what to say because he believed it.

I believed him. We would try again.

Summer came and it was swimming and T-shirts and peaches and yabbying in the creek and cricket and clover and bee-stings and exploring on the bikes and going on great adventures along the Goulburn River. And you never thought of football.

And then there was mention of it in the newspaper and on telly and, as autumn took hold, there'd be a few more mentions and soon you were living for Geelong again, without having to think about it. You had no idea of what this meant. You just followed Geelong because you loved Geelong.

I remember one of the early games that season. Dad had to drive all the way to Tarrington, near Hamilton in western Victoria, to be guest preacher for their Mission Festival. I went with him.

We are in the Morris 1100, which has no radio. Just me and Dad. We have the wireless with us but there is too much interference when the motor is running so I can't listen while Dad is driving. But I still try. I imagine that I can make out a commentator's voice amid the barking static. I listen until my ear hurts. I hope the coverage will improve. I believe it will improve. Every now and then we stop to get a score. We lean over the bonnet together trying to get the dial on a productive frequency. We find one as the broadcast goes around the grounds. Geelong is leading Carlton by three goals at quarter time. This is great. I am helping Dad to do his important work and the Cats are winning. We stop again. Geelong still leads. A little further up the road and we check the score. Me and Dad trying to find another station. Geelong just a couple of points ahead. We get to Tarrington. Geelong has lost. My eyes mist up. It feels like the season is over. Dad takes church the next day.

I was becoming a more sophisticated footy fan. On Friday mornings I'd race out and collect the *Sun* from the dewy front lawn, grab the milk, and get the crusty bread from the meter box. I'd take a bite from the corner, put it on the bench in the kitchen and then climb back into bed to read the League teams. The end of my bed would be a haven for the golden leaves which had stuck to my wet feet. I loved when the Geelong team had in bold letters beneath it: NO CHANGE. As if all was well with the world.

On Friday night we would watch 'Focus on Football' on ABC Channel 3 with Thorold Merrett, Percy Beames and Chicken Smallhorn who was so perfectly named because he looked very much like a wizened American Indian. We so wanted them to tip Geelong. Dad would come in from the study with an apple or an orange and take out his ancient pocketknife, so old the bone had fallen from the handle and the blade had nearly been worn away from years of sharpening. We would watch as he peeled the orange in one single peel holding up the length of skin, a great orange helix. He'd flick off the white bits on the outside and then he'd put a nick in the top which would allow him to break the orange apart. 'Who wants the navel?' he'd say. 'It's the best bit.' And we'd sit around sharing that single orange. Or an apple from which he'd cut a small piece and hand it to you on his knife. This would only occur while the panel analysed less significant games. None of Dad's tricks could distract us when Geelong was being discussed. Anyway, when it was Geelong, he was listening.

Going to sleep on Friday was a treat because you knew that when you woke up it would be Saturday. But then Saturday morning took forever to pass. First I'd check the sports section of the paper to see which radio stations were covering which games. I always hoped that the ABC had the Geelong game—that was the station we picked up best in Shepparton—although I was frustrated by the ABC's coverage because it had the horse races as well. When Doug Wade was about to kick for goal a voice would break in: 'They're moving in at Caulfield.' Then I'd check to see who Lou Richards had tipped. ('Dad, what's the Kiss of Death?') And then the kids' club pages. Then lunch.

I have a strong memory of the agonising wait of the last hour. I am in shorts and a T-shirt even though the April sunshine is weak and the wind has a sharp edge. Everyone else is inside. I've had enough of kicking the footy. It sits over by the jasmine which grows up the side of the garage. There is washing on the line. Time slows. I'm cold. I'm so cold I have to try to get warm but I can't be bothered going inside to get a jumper so I lie curled up inside the big tractor tube. Its black rubber holds the heat. It is warm. I try to maximise my contact with it. I look up as the clouds scutter across the blue sky.

I dream of a Geelong win. I don't wonder why. I just dream. I want them to win more than I want anything. I imagine passages of play which result in Doug Wade kicking for goal. I am still not warm enough. I have goose pimples on my legs. I coax the cat to come over. When he does I try to get him to lie on my legs like a blanket. He runs away. I try to imagine the scoreboard at the end of the game. I am still waiting. The clock has nearly stopped. When will the game finally start? I go inside and ask Mum, 'Can we have a fire?' and she says, 'You can't light the fire until you've put a jumper on.' (Team rules: like kicking to the top of the square from the dead pocket.) There's some pop-music show on TV: blokes with funny haircuts sing some sad song about Jude which I know is a book of the Bible. The show finishes and there is a brief cross to Arden Street or Victoria Park or the MCG where commentators do a preview, and just when the game looks like it's about to start the coverage finishes. We have to turn on our radio. Why? Team rules in Victoria: no live telecasts of football. It makes no sense to an eight-year-old.

We had one of those Ming dynasty radiograms, orangey-walnut in colour with a turntable and double doors, and those nylon speakers across the bottom that had that fabric with sparkly flecks. The radio had all the stations written on the plastic front; a layer for each state, even Tasmania. The sound it produced was one of the wonders of modern science; so rich and deep in a way that filled the whole house with footy commentary. That was if you were on a local station where the reception was good. We lived on the extreme limit of Melbourne radio stations' range so that if Geelong was playing Fitzroy on 3KZ we were in for a frustrating afternoon.

The aerial of the radiogram was a piece of co-axial cable. We worked out that if you exposed some of the wire on each side and wound the two sets of wires together and held the combined cable tightly between your fingers the reception improved at least enough to hear—amid the snow and static—that '3KZ *is* football' and that the match was brought to you by Radio Rentals ('Phone eight seven eight dub-late dub-late'). The reception always failed just as they were crossing to get the score at Kardinia Park. Often the static was so bad that the signal would disappear for a couple of minutes. Then it would come good just as a goal had been scored but you didn't know by whom. So you had to wait in this state of hope–fear—and then you'd punch the air when you learned it was another goal to the Cats.

I loved when they went around the grounds, the noise of the crowd in the background and the short sharp score from the voice of a former footballer: 'Fifteen and a half minute mark: Hawthorn 11.19, Footscray 12.12.' And then to the next ground where the tone of the crowd was different. You could imagine what was happening from just six seconds of live cross. In the instant before the voice gave the score there would be just enough information from the background noise to form an idea of what was going on: the roar of a goal, the single shriek of the woman not far from the commentary box at Vic Park who didn't want Des Tuddenham to be tackled; the rise and fall of the voices as someone flew and failed to latch onto a screamer; the chant of 'Rich-*mond* clap-clap-clap. Rich-*mond* clap-clap-clap' which suggested the Tiges were coming back; the collective cry of '*Ball!*'

I loved how two hundred games in the VFL meant that the round-the-grounds blokes knew when something was important enough for them to include it: 'Cowboy Neale's got his fifth,' during a second quarter cross; 'Jesaulenko's down and I reckon they've called for the stretcher.' And when the situation was critical at another venue, they would just cut across the main broadcast: 'North have hit the front,' or 'Another goal to Hudson. Scores are level, Harry.' I knew what all this meant. I knew this language. Nothing compared to this excitement.

Sometimes the static would be just too much and the voices would be lost and I'd find that I'd been hanging on so tight that the copper wire had disintegrated between my fingers and I'd have to call Dad to pare a bit more of the plastic back. He'd come out of the study filling his pipe with Dr Pat and put his pocketknife to work.

Many of these great matches I visualised in my mind. They became imagined contests with all of the action and colour generated by nothing more than the commentary and the sound effects mike, and of course by the fact that footy was a cracker of a game. Saturday afternoon was wonderful.

At half time, if it wasn't raining, I would ask Dad to come outside and kick the footy. Kicking the footy with Peter and David wasn't really kicking the footy because they were too small. Even if it was misty, Dad would find ten minutes and you would wind up with droplets of water in your hair and a red-brown mark on your chest. And you'd come back inside in time for the third quarter and Mum would bake pikelets and scones which were warm and covered with homemade blood plum jam and Mum would always say, 'They're a bit cloonchy' which was a word used in our household for doughy scones and dumplings in Kloesse soup and then you'd listen to the rest of the footy.

If Geelong won a close one there'd be lots of fist-clenching and the shouting of 'Yes!' If they won easily there'd be lots of nodding and acknowledgment that we had a great team and that you would expect little else and that really it was never in doubt. If they lost there was always that same horrible feeling that only time could alleviate and then that encouraging word from Dad or Mum—'They'll play better next week.'

After the radio broadcast was finished we waited for 'Today's Football' and then 'League Replay'. We always ate together at the kitchen table—except when the footy was on. They were great times, watching the black-and-white coverage of the last quarter of Geelong games. Mum would make her own sausage rolls, and the flaky pastry and tomato sauce made a paste that the world's greatest chefs will never emulate. Sometimes it would be hot dogs: frankfurts on toast so that the melted butter and sauce ran down your arm.

We would know the result, yet we would cheer every Geelong goal. I remember one monumental match against Collingwood. Geelong is five goals down at three-quarter time and the Magpies have played like the thugs they really are. These were the days when one of the trickiest philosophical questions for Victorians was whether they loved their own team more than they hated Collingwood. We loved Geelong more. Collingwood have resorted to their usual violent tactics to even up the imbalance in skill and Geelong is left with only seventeen players. But we are not defeated. We lift. A goal. And another one. The Cats are fighting back. Another. We know the result but somehow we are so locked into the situation that we forget, or deny it, and we are still hopeful. It's time-on and the Cats are going forward. Another goal. We trail by four points. The crowd is in a frenzy as the umpires return the ball to the middle. Paper flies everywhere: streamers, cut-up newspaper, toilet paper, cut-up phone books. The paper of ordinary life. The commentators are thinking that this is a great game; a great moment in the history of the Geelong Football Club; of football, of the state of Victoria. Although I don't have the words to express it somewhere inside me I feel that this will be a victory for goodness. I yell for Geelong. I yell for justice. Justice will prevail. This will never be forgotten. The Cats go forward again. They give everything. The ball comes into full forward. This is our last chance. There's a scramble, but Collingwood clears. They race through the centre. Goal. The commentator barks, 'That's the sealer. And they can thank their lucky stars, the Magpies, that they've got out of this one.' Collingwood win by ten points. Geelong is brave in defeat.

Even Mum has watched.

Sunday had a feel of its own. It was a special day: the day we went to church and the day we watched 'World of Sport'. These two institutions kept the earth spinning safely on its axis.

After breakfast we got ready for Sunday School. I wore a bow tie and pulled my pants up too high (apparently). We had to find our text cards from the previous Sunday and stick them in our text card books. Someone would yell, 'Where's the Clag?' Then we had to learn our texts so we could recite them to our teachers.

Church followed Sunday School at 11 a.m. The problem was that 'World of Sport' started at midday. We prayed for short sermons. If Dad preached for too long from the pulpit there was a chance we'd miss the first part of the show and that could mean not seeing Mark of the Day, one of the highlights of the Victorian week. Communion services were even more trouble because it took such a long time to get everyone through. After Communion Mum would return to our pew clutching her handkerchief and smelling of ruby port. As the organist continued to play 'O Sacred Head Now Wounded' she would bow her head in a moment of quiet prayer. Sometimes she would look sad. But we hardly noticed. We just wanted everything to finish.

We didn't have watches. We didn't need them. You could feel when 'World of Sport' started. If Dad had got carried away we would wait for the end of the Benediction and then ask Mum if we could leave during the last hymn. Usually we stayed to hear the organ's rich harmonies and to sing one of the doxologies (which we liked because they were short and signified the end) from the Lutheran Hymnal. My favourite was sung to Haydn's 'Austria' (the German national anthem):

> Worship, honour, glory, blessing,
> Lord, we offer to Thy name;
> Young and old, thy praise expressing,
> Join their Saviour to proclaim.
> As the saints in heaven adore Thee,
> We would bow before Thy throne;
> As Thine angels serve before Thee,
> So on earth Thy will be done.

Then we waited for Dad to do the announcements: ('Divine service will be held, God willing, next Sunday at 11 a.m.' It was always, 'God willing'). I would leave feeling uplifted as if all were well with the world. Then I'd run back to the manse—spirit nourished—put the telly on, and stoke the fire.

Dad and Mum would return about half an hour later after chatting with the parishioners and Dad would be relieved to find out that Mark of the Day hadn't been on. We would sit in the warm lounge room and hang on every word about Geelong as if it should be recorded with a big swirly first letter on the page of the new week.

We eat lunch—or dinner, as we called it—in front of the telly. The fire flickers behind the glass door. I stand in front of it with my hands behind my back enjoying the warm air from the fan. Dad is sprawled out on a chair. He is drained. Mum gets everything ready. The characters on 'World of Sport' chat away. They are like figures from the Old Testament. Bob Davis explains how crook the umpiring was at Kardinia Park, and Jack Dyer argues with Lou Richards. And that bloke does ads. And the woodchop. And the handball. And the kick. And Bruce Andrew, looking like something out of the 1930s. And you always want it to be a Geelong player. And you wish Bill Collins would just get off because horse-racing is such a waste of time. And Mum serves stew with potatoes and carrots and onion—with mashed potato. We sprinkle Worcestershire sauce over it. There is lots of thick white bread to mop up the gravy.

I can't eat stew without being returned to those days. This was my religious experience.

We lived opposite a vacant allotment: the place where the neighbourhood built its Cracker Night bonfire. Cracker Night made us feel a bit British and glad to be part of the Commonwealth. It was one of those festival days like Anzac Day, the Melbourne Cup, the Bathurst 500, the Stawell Gift or the Edinburgh Military Tattoo. Football was different: it was routinely significant, like church. All year people would drag bits of timber, old tyres, anything that would add to the community flame and satisfy the tendency towards pyromania. Part of the allotment had been sold and a milk bar was built at one end. The owner had paid strict attention to the rules of milk bars: in the window was the mandatory Coca-Cola and *Sun* advertising, Pura milk and Tarax signs. Inside, it smelt like all corner stores smell south of the Murray: as if a Victorian milk bar licence comes with an aerosol can which is sprayed around so that a milk bar at Lakes Entrance smells exactly like one in Warracknabeal—an olfactory *je ne sais quoi* with a hint of pie-warmer and loose lollies (jelly babies two for one cent, cobbers one cent each, raspberries two for one cent, sherbies two for one cent, mint leaves two for one cent, bullets two for one cent) and Big Charlies and a jar of snowballs next to the cash register. In those days every milk bar had a jar of snowballs—and a jar of those marshmallowy things stuck between two very yellow wafers. Our milk bar owner was pretty switched on. He won instant loyalty by giving everybody a candy cane in their club colours thereby having us all associate his shop with our great passion.

He also stocked footy cards. This created a difficult situation, if not a moral dilemma, in our home. Mum and Dad were happy for us to enjoy the memorabilia that fell out of cereal packets but one of their greatest parenting challenges was that the very best footy cards came with chewing gum. In 1970 chewing gum was up there with Sunday sport and Mao Tse-tung.

No amount of explaining that it was the cards we wanted and not the chewy would sway Mum's tough stance. But we must have pestered her hard. I was grateful for the loophole which allowed her to adjust her conscience to permit us to spend some of our pocket money on this great pleasure although we were made to feel it was an incredible indulgence. This made the cards all the more valuable. We even went in search of empty bottles down by the river to make some cash.

It was a thrill to buy Scanlen's footy cards at that milk bar. They cost five cents. You would get a thin packet of five cards wrapped in waxed paper with that powdery stuff—and two sticks of pink chewy. You would look at those cards hoping that you didn't have them or if you did you knew someone else who didn't and was looking to swap. Scanlen's footy cards had a portrait of the player within a TV set and underneath was a football-shaped bubble which named his club and position. There were some classic poses: the one-handed pick-up on the run while looking at the camera; the baulk with the arm fully outstretched; the grinning rover taking a chest mark. These shots were taken at training in very poor light. They exude an innocence; as if the marketers at Scanlen's were still actually bringing you a portrait of a VFL footballer rather than selling bubble gum. There were even a few where the players were setting up for the place kick which even then was all but extinct. The drop kick was about to appear in the endangered species gazette. Laid out, the back of the cards made up the final scoreboard of the 1969 VFL grand final. We had the whole set except one. I managed to lose those cards many years later when shifting house as a student.

There were also footy cards in Sunicrust bread, but we weren't a packaged-bread family. We were a baker's-bread-in-the-meter-box family. But we did convince Mum to buy a few loaves of Sunicrust to get the cartoon cards which pictured common footy sayings like 'In the van' and 'Looks like Tarzan, plays like Jane' and 'Mollydooker' and 'Suspended player'. They were funny if you were seven.

We spent ages playing kick-to-kick in the yard: backwards and forwards and backwards and forwards with Peter and David and sometimes a few mates. Our footy was getting old but we kept it in good nick. We used brown Nugget and kept it pumped up. It was entitled to be showing signs of wear. Other kids brought their footies: some were roundish, some were split along the stitching, some had little rubber hernias where the bladder pushed through, some had lost the leather lacing and were opening at the top to reveal the valve, some had a mysterious object inside them which rattled, some were yellow, some were in club colours, some were synthetic. The older ours got the more it tended towards the round but it was leather and it still had enough balance to spin on its two axes. Footies were amazing things. They alerted you to a sense of perfection. What was truer and more beautiful than a sweetly timed drop kick? They also alerted you to a sense of chaos. What was more chaotic than the wobble of a torp that's gone off the side of the boot? Sometimes they were so predictable. Why did they bounce end on end: two low forward bounces and then on the third they'd sit up on their point and bounce high. Often they gave you no chance. Why did they sometimes bounce any which way and no matter how closely you watched them you could never pick it?

I loved sinking the boot into the footy. I could kick a drop kick. When Dad kicked one he looked like an old-fashioned footballer who just let the ball fall onto his foot. I used the modern Billy Goggin or Billy Barrot method. They sort of raised the nose of the ball and placed it down onto their feet. I wasn't always as successful as they were. Sometimes I would kick too close to the end of the ball and it would spin fast like the back rotor on a helicopter and have very little momentum. Sometimes it would just skew off. But just occasionally you would get it right—your foot, the ground and the ball would meet in unison—and the footy would spin at the perfect rate and sail forever.

I could also kick a drop punt. I started out using the Robert Walls technique but gradually developed more of a Peter McKenna method with cocked wrists and my middle fingers down the seam on either side of the footy.

And then there was the torp. Dad called it a 'screwy'. He didn't kick it like the players on TV. He placed his hand under the ball and dropped it onto his foot. I wanted to kick a torp like Doug Wade did on TV but my hands weren't big enough so I used to hold the ball on the side and lay it across my foot. Sometimes its spiral would pierce the air and it would fly over the head of the pack at the other end. To get any distance I had to time it perfectly.

In grade three you got to play in your first official footy matches—at the lightning carnival for grade threes. Boys used to look forward to this day like they would to their first communion. For me this was going to be the start of a 600-game career (330 of which were going to be for the Geelong Football Club). I would play twenty-five games a year for twenty-five years—at least. But life hasn't taken me that way and I have played so little football in the past thirty years that not only can I remember individual matches, I can remember individual pieces of play and my role in them, however minor.

On the day of that lightning carnival we don't go

into class. We get the bus. The carnival takes all day. Dad comes to watch our first match which is probably why the teacher in charge gives me a run. I am a particularly small child. In fact I'm puny. I get stuck in other people's cars because I'm not strong enough to pull up the plastic stem locks on the doors. I live in constant fear that Miss Phillips will ask me to clean the blackboard—I can't push down hard enough to do anything but smear chalk across the board. Dad says I've got biceps like a chicken's instep. One time when we are visiting our cousins I find a chest expander: it has handles and three springs joining them. I try to pull it apart and cannot move it at all. I put one handle on the floor and put my foot in it like a stirrup. I grab the other handle and pull up as hard as I can with both hands and it moves a little bit but my foot slips and the handle flies up and smashes into my jaw. It knocks me over. I'm a bit wobbly when I get up. I don't tell anyone I've been bashed up by a chest expander.

I really want to play footy—more than just about everything. I want so much to run bravely onto the oval and to not be frightened and intimidated. I want to look the barking dogs from the opposing side sternly in their Rottweiler eyes. But they are big and they can kick forever. They joke with each other before the game while I wonder whether my double knot is tight enough or if I should ask the coach to do it up for me again.

Just on half time in our first match I find myself

running towards a loose ball. It is about to cross the boundary line. I sense footsteps behind me and stop and let my opponent bump into my back. Throwing myself forward face first in the finest tradition of Kevin Bartlett, I hear the umpire's whistle. I have milked my first free kick (I really did have Geelong in my blood) and I am not far from the point post. As a scholarly eight-year-old I remember going back and thinking that I am on the wrong side for a right footer—and then the bell goes. At twelve metres from goal I'm probably too far out to score. I immediately consider my reference point—'League Replay'. What would they do on TV? So in the finest tradition of after-siren dobs, I go the torp. I put in all my effort but I produce one of those hooks that spins like a drop punt and it lands about nine and a half metres away at the top of the square.

I must have rushed it because Dad comes over and, as we walk towards the half time huddle, he says, 'You don't have to hurry. Next time you get a free kick, just take your time.' To which I reply, 'Dad, I think they pump the footballs up too hard here.'

Later that day I am playing on the wing and the ball comes over to me and one of our players scoops it up and I yell at him, 'You're clear, you're clear, you're clear' (the coach has said it's very important to be your team-mates' eyes and to talk to each other and tell them when they're clear) and I run alongside him with my arms outstretched in the classic 1970 grade three shepherding position. I look like a motorbike cop trying to protect the cavalcade during the Queen's visit. I am faster than he is so I get well in front of him, but I slow down so he can catch up. I don't call for the hand-ball. He kicks for goal. He misses. The ball comes to me again and I try to kick it to my full forward or, more accurately, to the kid standing further up the ground and my very best pass misses the target by yards but bounces forever and rolls through for a point. I can't remember how we fared but we have played footy and it is a bit rough but it is the greatest thing I know. All I want to do is play footy and I don't know if I can.

Like Geelong. They couldn't do it in 1970. They finished fifth. Carlton won the great grand final. I didn't take too much notice at the time. I have watched the famous game many times since.

CHAPTER 3

It rains a lot in Victoria. When I was kid it rained a lot more. They were the days when around the Queen's Birthday weekend every year a great big low pressure would park itself over Glenferrie Oval and wouldn't move until the second-last round. On some ovals the puddles would never dry up. They'd have tadpoles in them and the only explanation for that rattle in the footy was that one of the tadpoles had got inside and turned into a frog. The turf was like chocolate mousse in places. I have heaps of photos of muddied VFL footballers, hair plastered to their heads by rain. I remember games where the ball would come to a complete stop in the middle of the Merri Creek gluepot.

We spent a lot of time inside. It would get dark very

early—not long after school—and we would sit in the cosy lounge room playing cards or Scrabble or Monopoly or I'd reread *Football the Australian Way* or my footy scrapbook. When I was in grade four it rained and rained. We watched lots of telly: 'The Flintstones', 'Hogan's Heroes' and our favourite, 'F-Troop'. Sometimes you could hear the rain on the roof and when it died down a bit you could hear the *ssshh* of tyres on the wet street. A rack of school clothes was set permanently in front of the fire, along with all the school shoes.

At school I could do most of the work without too much trouble. A few things bothered me. I used to get some of my times tables wrong because I'd think in terms of footy scores. I used to think 9x7 was 61, and 8x8 was 56, and 7x6 was 48. I knew footy scores. I thought about footy scores. I liked how some dates were actually footy scores—like 11 May 1971 was 11.5.71.

I had an idea of typical scores. I thought 5.2.32 to 2.3.15 was the quintessential quarter-time score and that the definitive full-time score was 15.12.102 to 13.13.91. I liked scores like 27.8.170 and I sort of liked it when Geelong kicked 15.2.92 that day against Richmond, although we led by four goals at three-quarter time and lost. I liked scores like 9.22.76 especially when kicked by North Melbourne and 9.24.78 when kicked by Collingwood. I liked those massive scores that they kicked in the VFA thirds. I would pore over the results looking for a

Coburg 69.42.456 to Yarraville 0.2.2. And I'd even read through the country footy results. I sort of had a team in every league.

But I knew that if I really wanted to be a footballer, I needed to join in with the footballers at school. So what if I could do it at home. I needed to go out on the main oval at the breaks with all the big grade fives and sixes and take part in footy as it was played at Gowrie Street State School.

There were no real rules but there were a few conventions. Everyone spread out within about forty metres of goal. A grade six kid kicked out from the goal square: the big kid who always had twenty cents to spend at the milk bar after school, and might give you a Samboy barbecue chip to keep you under his spell. He was good at that. The others would try and scunge a Fruit Tingle off him and he'd tell them to nick off and make them feel like idiots for asking even though the day before he'd have walked up and given them one. This is the nature of a reign of terror. He wasn't a bad kick though. His technique was wrong but he was big enough to get some distance. There'd be a bit of a marking contest and a scramble on the ground and someone would wind up in possession. A passage of play would follow. Those close to the ball then decided whether they were going to be team-mates of the kid in possession, or defenders.

Roles were pretty clearly defined. There was one group that always attacked. It was characterised by its members' ability to cover one nostril and blow snot onto the ground. It was led by Bomber and Datta and some of the other toughs who dominated the game and were certain to play key positions in the school team and one day be asked to try out in Melbourne. The defenders tended to be kids who actually brought a hanky to school and were almost certainly looking forward to a career on the half forward flank or goal umpiring.

It was one-way traffic. You could risk ridicule by running past and calling for a handball from one of them. Or you could risk a smack in the mouth if you went in too hard to tackle. You couldn't tackle Datta anyway. He was an Aboriginal lad with long skinny legs and he ran with Cathy Freeman's stride. He kicked with his left foot; beautiful raking grade six kicks that hit his mates on the chest or went through post high. He had footy in him.

I wasn't one of the tough kids' mates. I had footy in me, too, but my footy was different from theirs. Theirs was *Clockwork Orange* football whereas mine was *Chitty Chitty Bang Bang*. For me, football was not about anger and violence and toughness and domination. It was more a glorious concept—an ongoing dream, a phantasmal reality, not necessarily tangible nor obviously real; and yet it was real.

I could do the tangible things—some of the things that made up football. I could mark and kick. But I didn't have the strength of the tough kids. I didn't have their aggression, or their brutality. And I didn't have their courage or cockiness. These were kids who said, 'Made yuh look'; kids who'd give you a Chinese burn; kids who drank school milk like the blokes in the VB ad downed beer. Then they'd wipe the white moustache off their faces. I needed to bring a little tin of strawberry Quik along to get it down at all. They scorned knuckles as a game of skill whereas I was happy to try it. I'm not sure what they thought of my willingness to join some of the girls in making daisy chains from those little yellow daisies, or of my enthusiasm for school work and library books like *Let's Visit Kenya* and *One Fish Two Fish Red Fish Blue Fish*.

If by some miracle the kick-out did fall to me, I knew that I was obliged to handball it to one of the usual attackers at once. I thought this was very unfair, but I knew there would be retribution if I didn't. One day I ran and took a bounce but I could hear the footsteps and the voice, 'I'm on yuh, I'm on yuh, I'm on yuh', and I had to dig deep to stop from looking around, from hunching my shoulders so that my neck disappeared, and from taking tiny steps.

But I was also earnest and often I'd call for the handball. 'Bomber, Bomber, goin' past, goin' past.' I was discouraged, if not hurt, when sometimes he'd laugh a laugh of contempt as if to say, 'What are you doing that for?' But the biggest laugh came when one day, to my surprise, Datta gave me the handball as I flew by, I ran into goal and from fifteen metres out on the slightest of angles hit the post. I slumped to my knees and skidded along with my hands covering my face. Everyone laughed and all the toughs slumped to their knees and put their hands over their faces. I felt I was in the wrong place. It was as if the world were for others.

Strangely, though, these experiences didn't deter me. I announced to Mum and Dad at the start of the 1971 season that I wanted to play for the Shepparton club. The youngest junior club was for Under-13s. I was eight. I must have been very keen because Dad and Mum agreed, and I found myself at training with kids from form I and II. I looked like the mascot who runs out with '½' on his back. But I used to do all the drills trying as hard as I could all of the time.

That year I wasn't selected until 4 June when I was named nineteenth man for the match against Mooroopna. This came as a shock to my parents who had reasonably assumed that I wouldn't get a game all season and had deferred the purchase of any proper footy shorts until the following season (or even the season after that).

There was panic that Saturday morning. Only one clothes store opened early enough. The only pair of footy shorts for sale would have looked at home on Carji Greeves. They were far too big and had adjustable side buckles which had to be pulled tight just to keep the shorts up—I looked like I was wearing a tennis skirt. I got to run around a little bit in the last quarter that day but failed to gather a possession. We won 10.11 to 2.4 but I didn't do enough to hold my place. Clearly my pointing and talking mustn't have satisfied the selectors because I wasn't picked again until 25 June when, according to the *Shepparton News*, I was named as eighth emergency. I wasn't named again for the rest of the season.

Most of the time I liked training although I got a little concerned when the coach made half of us take our shirts off for a game of handball keepings off. It was the dead of winter and I was cold. The wet, heavy ball also hurt my punching hand so Dad showed me how to handball with the heel of my hand. No one else hand-balled like that. The coach was kind. He was very encouraging—and tolerant, having to put up with some crackpot kid who was there three years before his time.

I took in all the trappings of club footy. Pie night was a new experience: big trays of pies that were just the right temperature. They tasted great. They tasted like football. And bottles of Tarax. We all wanted to get each of the letters inside the bottle tops to win the prize. The other boys wolfed down pie after pie but it took me ages to eat just one and I sort of sat watching everyone else as they laughed and punched each other and farted and told stupid jokes.

Being a club footballer who didn't play wasn't all bad. It allowed me to follow Geelong on the radio or go to the Basin Reserve or Princes Park to watch the Saturday afternoon matches in the local Goulburn Valley League. Dad even took us up to Kyabram early in the season. He wanted us to see Fred Wooller who was seeing out his final years there as the captain-coach. Dad explained that Fred Wooller had been captain of Geelong's premiership side in 1963. Wow. The Kyabram ground was packed; it was a sea of red and black and white floppy hats in the sunshine. Everyone was enjoying themselves. It was like a Sunday School picnic—only much bigger. And we got to see a real live Geelong player.

Even though I played for Shepparton I didn't really barrack for any team in the local competition. We had a soft spot for Mooroopna, however, because they wore Geelong colours. One rainy afternoon we went to see them play. We sat in the car and shared a Cherry Ripe and tooted when Mooroopna kicked a goal but really we concentrated on the VFL scores on the wireless, as did many others sitting in their cars.

Sometimes I'd go to the footy by myself. I'd ride the back way along the Goulburn River to Princes Park, where we did Little Athletics in the summer. It was a beautiful ground, set low in the flood flat and surrounded by imposing gum trees. Sounds reverberated in the natural amphitheatre.

I remember afternoons of footy there. The local community gathered to watch the match between Shepparton and Lemnos: plumbers and builders and dairy farmers in Stetsons drinking beers; accountants and auctioneers in tweed jackets; Italian fruit-block owners with hairy arms and shiny pates; mums and dads and grandpas and nannas; girlfriends with too much make-up and pregnant wives and kids with ten cent's worth of mixed lollies and a footy under their arm.

Lots of people sit in their cars parked around the fence. I sit on one of the weathered forms along the wing. I hope I don't get a splinter and that the rain stays away. The players run out: clean and neat and glistening and smelling of liniment, running together in a big pack, jogging and surging and then doing a few drills with the footballs. The captains toss: Shepparton have the breeze. The players rub turf between their hands as they walk to their positions. They find their opponents. Most shake hands. Some bump shoulders, some chest each other, some are angry. There is a bit of a blue. Other players run over wondering, as they are running over, whether to pull the fight apart or go the big haymaker. Then things settle and the umpire nods to the respective captains. He raises the ball aloft. The car horns sound and the siren goes and he thumps the ball into the cricket pitch. You can hear the thump all around the ground, even above the car horns. And the game is under way. The first ten minutes are furious, all whistles and voices and the smack of contesting bodies and cheers and horns, and then it becomes quieter as fewer people toot after a goal.

At quarter time I jump the fence and join all the men in the Shepparton huddle. Blokes use their football voices. 'Come on fellas,' they say. 'We can beat this mob. They got nothin'. They're gutless.' Players mill around. They swig water and break from the huddle to spit it on the ground. After a while the coach calls them together. He speaks calmly, 'Look, fellas, we're up. That's fine. But we're not thinking. We're going too short and too wide. Far too bloody wide. Fellas, we talked about this before the game. What did we say? Straight up the guts. Simmo's the best centre half forward goin' round. Their bloke can't get near him. And whatta we do? We ignore him. Come on, fellas. Kick it long to him. We want it in there while he's got a bitta space. Billy and Killer, stay outta there. Let him go one on one. Then hit the pack. Hit it late.' He pauses to gather his thoughts and some Italian builder pipes up like Chico Marx, 'Hey. Come onna Shep.'

The coach continues, 'Robbo, yuh gotta get tighter mate. Don't let him wander into their forward line. Macca, in front. We gotta be first to the ball. Show them yuh want it. Make them think they're not gunna get an easy one all day. And Wes. Where's Wes? No fuckin' speccies.' Only Wes isn't there to hear him because he's broken away from the huddle to catch the eye of the bird he's picked up at the Criterion the night before, and he's saying g'day. The coach builds them up and there are the appropriate urgings and voices affirming the commitment to effort in the second quarter, until they finish with the big 'C'arn Shep!' Then they break, and what was a tight, close group is all over the place. The coach takes one more player aside for a chat and other players have their own conversations as they walk to the back line. They may be talking about footy—they might also be talking about fruit fly.

I try to find someone with a radio so I can overhear a Geelong score. I walk around the ground watching the game. Shepparton dominate. They are all over the opposition. They pile on the goals.

At half time I follow the Lemnos players into the dressing room. I love the sound of their boots on the concrete. They are a few goals down. They have mud on them and grass and red marks. They smell of effort. They need more liniment. One has a trickle of blood on his eyebrow. They suck on pieces of orange and drink from old Cottees bottles. Some have towels. Each is self-absorbed partly because he's buggered and partly because he's thinking about what's just happened out there and what his contribution has been. But they're mostly buggered.

I sit between two huge blokes. I am about nine. Tiny. No one minds that I'm sitting there. They don't even notice me. They are wet. A smoke gets passed around. They don't say much. They sit with toothless grimaces looking like Kevin Murray: warhorses who've played footy for years. Fat trainers rub more liniment into fatigued muscles.

The captain-coach maintains an air of confidence. He talks with the runner and with a bloke in a coat and tie. He refuses to show any sign of physical strain even though he's played on the ball for most of the first half and has kept Lemnos in it. I swing my legs like I do in church. The coach speaks to them again. I listen. He's pleased that no one has stopped chasing. He says that there will be reward for effort. Lemnos can win.

They try hard after the break but Shep hold them out and at three-quarter time I join their huddle. There are sprig marks all over the oval. The huddle is much bigger and the situation more urgent. The players mill around: the reliable full back, a thirty-four-year-old dairy farmer with immaculate Californian Poppy hair; the Greek rover, socks down to reveal legs like Corinthian columns; the eccentric in a brand of boots never before seen in Shepparton; the stud—a Tom Selleck–Sam Newman hybrid —with the moustache and the Monaro and the denim shirt and tight jeans; the red-headed teacher on country service; the ento-mologist from the DPI who wears long sleeves and brings his gear to the ground in a Gladstone bag; the barrel-chested enforcer with the tattoo; the racehorse, a young skinny flanker whose white ankle supports make him look like a Hoysted two-year-old; the young fellow who's just back from Vietnam; the flea-like Aboriginal forward pocket with bum-fluff on his chin whose jumper is too big and hangs under his armpits and who flies for huge marks over the top of the stud; his cousin who no one can tackle; two blokes in dressing gowns. This disparate lot had somehow came together in common purpose.

Lemnos are five goals down but they have shown plenty in the third quarter and they've got the wind in the last. There is a real feeling in the huddle that they can come back. A belief. Almost a knowledge.

The players have gathered in tight. They are arm in arm. You could cover them all with a chenille bedspread. The coach times his last words: 'We've gotta go out there and give everything. I don't fuckin' care if we walk off on the wrong side of the scoreboard. We've gotta get out there and give it a fair dinkum go.'

'Yeah. C'mon. We can do this.'

'We've gotta walk off with nothin' left in the tank. We've gotta be able to walk off with a bitta pride. We've gotta be able to walk off with our heads up.'

'C'mon Lemnos.' The focus is intense.

'We're right in this fellas—if you believe we are. Five goals—so what? We kicked five goals in eight minutes at Euroa. I know we've got that in us. I fuckin' know we have.'

'Course, we have. C'arn fellas. C'arn Lemnos.'

'We can win this fellas. We've worked for this. We've worked hard. Together. Fellas, ask yourself: what does the bloke standin' next to you mean to you? Ask yourself: what does this jumper mean to you? What does the Lemnos footy club mean to you?'

'Yeah!' For a moment, this is a brotherhood.

'Let's get out there and show them what Lemnos is all about.'

The coach's climax is supported by a great guttural

affirmation; a liturgical response. Everyone is pumped. The tribe disperses: players stride purposefully to position and the drinkers purposefully to the bar.

I sit behind the goalposts at the Lemnos end. They start winning the footy in the middle. The full forward leads and marks. He puts it through. Then they get another one. Back in the centre, the Georgie Bisset rover breaks clear and bombs it in to full forward; a huge kick from a little man. The full forward and the full back wrestle. The ball is in the air forever. They wind up sprawled on the ground. The footy sails through. The car horns sound wildly. Lemnos clear from the backline. The ball is roosted high to centre half forward. The full forward decides early he can get to the contest. He sprints. He launches himself; knee on the shoulder. His momentum and the lift of the pack carry him impossibly high. He is way above the pack, so high that he can mark on his chest. He does. His feet bicycle kick on the way down in an attempt to keep his balance. He hits the ground. Players stop and shake their heads. Horns toot. I cheer. The crowd senses it has seen something great. The full forward picks himself up. His face is blank. He goes back and thumps it through again. I find myself clapping, drawn in by the Lemnos spirit.

Lemnos win the ball in the centre again. The full forward leads straight up the middle. He's too early and too quick. His opponent is with him. They fly for the footy together and it glances off their hands and bobbles around in the worn goal square. The little forward pocket player runs at it and throws out a boot. Off the ground. He connects brilliantly. The goal umpire pulls his bum back as it flies past. Goal. The footy smashes into a car. I am so close I am splattered with mud, the sour turf which has endured the season's traffic. Lemnos have hit the front. They are unstoppable. They run away with the game.

I love footy.

I ride my bike home. It is just on dark. Mum says, 'How was the football?'

I say, 'Pretty good.'

CHAPTER 4

It seems ridiculous when I think about it now, but the first VFL games I saw in Melbourne were Collingwood games. I desperately wanted to go to a Geelong game but it was too difficult for Dad to give up a Saturday— he had to write his sermon and get ready for church on Sunday.

I had a friend, Craig Hogan, from Little Athletics. He was from a family who were all Collingwood members. His was an unusual Collingwood family in that there were no immediate relatives in jail. The Hogans went to most games. Often his sisters didn't want to go and on occasions they'd invite me. I remember the first time.

I am dropped off at the Hogans and I have been

given some money. I am thrilled to be going to the footy but am also a little apprehensive. I don't know what to expect. I don't know whether Mr Hogan and his mate will be mean and horrible or whether they'll be nice. At the Hogans' the girls are playing records and dancing. They are dressed up in Saturday morning dancing gear. They have friends over. They just keep dancing. They are girls.

We drive to Melbourne. The Hogans have a car radio so we can listen to the previews—Collingwood–Fitzroy, Geelong–Carlton. It is round four and the Maggies haven't been beaten. I keep an eye out for those white distance posts which tell us how far to go. It is 1971 but in some ways we are closer to the nine-teenth century than the twenty-first. We slow down at the old black-and-white 35 mph signs. Kids play footy on the ovals in the country towns. We get into Melbourne and drive through streets I didn't know existed. We park in Collingwood. There are funny little houses and gummy ladies in aprons lean their bosom on the fence and say g'day to those walking past. We get to Victoria Park. There are people everywhere; meeting, talking, selling *Footy Records* (Mr Hogan buys us one), selling pies and drinks, selling badges. I am like Oliver Twist in London. Perhaps someone will start singing 'Consider Yourself'. Only I'm not at home; I'm in Collingwood and urchins here look like they'd have you. They have freckles and wear the club's colours: duffel coats with number 6 on the back, scarves and sleeveless footy jumpers over the top of other jumpers. I have no idea of the rivalry between these two clubs. I have no idea of the geography of Melbourne. I hardly grasp the idea that these clubs represent a place, a people, a way of life. In my mind Geelong is a footy team, not a city an hour's drive from Melbourne. Somehow Geelong and Lemnos are very different entities.

We find our seats in the sunshine. Mr Hogan and his mate disappear for the last quarter of the reserves. I have to be careful not to lose my money. Craig and I have a pie. The crowd builds. I am sitting with real people. There is a huge cheer as Collingwood comes onto the ground. These are the players I have watched on telly all these years. They are real as well. I have a weird feeling. I am somehow removed from all of this. It's as if I should hold up a piece of cardboard with a rectangular hole in it to give my view a frame; a border like a TV screen's. But I love the noise. I love the feeling. I spot the players I know: McKenna, Richardson, Dean, Tuddenham for Collingwood and Murray and Ruscuklic for Fitzroy. Collingwood dominate. It is fast and skilful. I can feel the adoration for Collingwood. The floggers salute another Collingwood goal. I am wise enough to keep my support of the Fitzroy Football Club to myself.

I check the letters that represent the other games on the scoreboard. I know about the letters because I've seen them on TV. I don't worry about the race results. McKenna boots one out of the ground. Geelong is keeping in touch with Carlton. At half time Mr Hogan and his mate duck off again. We talk with some old people next to us. They are as old as our grandparents and they like us. They smile and they are probably remembering when they were young. They buy us each a soft drink.

I have to go to the toilet. I am worried. The toilet is full of blokes shuffling along. I stand waiting. It smells like the dunnies at school. Individual voices break the half quiet. 'Go you Woodsmen,' and 'C'arn Pies.' They have the *Record* under one arm and put their cans on the bench above the porcelain urinal. One bloke farts, a long fart and half turns his head so his chin is on his shoulder and says, 'You gotta give her some choke, fellas.'

Collingwood is too strong for the Royboys. Geelong loses to Carlton. We walk back to the car. The Fitzroy people walk despondently. They talk. What can be done? The Collingwood people are full of life. We drive home listening to the post-match analysis on the radio. The sunshine has turned to rain. It gets heavier. I sit in the back watching the raindrops coming straight at the windscreen in the headlights. They hypnotise me and I am in this dreamy world which relives the day.

Peter and David and I put more and more pressure on Mum and Dad to take us to a Geelong game, until at last they agreed. We go to the Geelong–Footscray game at Waverley. It is the middle of winter: overcast and windy and cold. We all go. Even Mum. We have plenty of goodies to eat. When we arrive Mum and Dad decide we should sit behind the goals. We are right behind the Geelong cheer squad. They are friendly. We are on their side. They talk to us. It's a huge ground. The Cats run out. We see our heroes live: Doug Wade, Billy Goggin, Bill Ryan, Sam Newman, Ian Nankervis, Gareth Andrews. This is really happening. We are really watching Geelong. We are very excited about the game starting and when it does things happen way up the other end of the ground which is good because it's the Geelong end. Still it's hard to see. We're in front. Please Geelong, win. We shiver.

In the second quarter we see more of the action but Footscray look like they might get back into the game. They do. The umpiring is shocking. The cheer squad starts to believe it can make a difference. Clap-clap. Clap-clap-clap. Clap-clap-clap-clap. '*Geelong*.' Over and over again. And we're joining in. Please, Geelong. A goal to Geelong and the floggers are waved and the cheer squad dance.

It's tight in the last quarter. All day Geelong has looked on top but we are in danger of losing. 'C'arn the Cats.' Footscray get a few goals clear coming into time-on. Everyone is screaming at the umpire. One of the cheer squad says he's hopeless. Another one calls him some words that we aren't allowed to say. We are screaming for Geelong to come back. They get one. The game becomes desperate. There are Geelong players running everywhere. Another goal to the Cats right in front of us. And we are jumping up and down and yelling at the tops of our voices. 'Gee-long clap-clap-clap. Gee-long clap-clap-clap.' Two points the difference. No one thinks about the cold. It's not cold. The ball comes our way again. The pack flies in the square. The Footscray defence jump on top of the ball. We scream '*Ball!*' The whistle blows. 'He's lying on it.' But it's a ball-up. 'No. No.' People throw their fists into the air. They hang over the fence and scream at the umpire. It can't be. 'He made no attempt, you idiot.'

One of the Doggies gets up. There's another defender over the ball. The Scraggers look sheepish. 'You're a gutless wonder, Deller.' The ball up is about five metres out. Rod Blake takes the ball out of the air just as Billy Goggin runs through. Blake gives a tiny, little handball. Goggin throws it on his boot. Goal. He flings his arms heavenward. 'It's a goal. He's put it through. We've won. We're home. The Cats are home. We've done it. We've done it.' It's pandemonium. We are jumping and hugging and cheering and screaming and clapping. But hang on. The umpire's pointing back to Gary Dempsey. It's a free kick. What for? Someone says he's called it a throw. The word is spread around. The balloon is pricked. There's boos and jeers and the umpire cops it. He is a white maggot, a white bastard, a cheating bastard and many other things that I don't understand.

The siren goes. We lose by two points. I look at Dad as if he can make things right; as if he has a way of alleviating injustice. It's horrible. It's shocking. We leave with the emptiest of feelings: as if our footy team has lost.

Later that year we saw Richmond beat Geelong at the MCG. It was cold and miserable and the Cats just weren't good enough. I had been to the MCG the summer before to see the test between Australia and England and I'd managed to get Colin Cowdrey's autograph. This time I jumped the fence and chased the nearest Geelong player. It was John Scarlett. He kept walking along while signing books until he stopped at the gate and was signing as many as he could. I got trampled in the rush. Bigger kids kept pushing me away. I didn't know you could do that. It wasn't fair. Why couldn't we all just take our turn? Then I got booted in the shin. It upset me. Not because it hurt but because I was kicked by another Geelong supporter. I felt wounded. I limped back across the MCG. I didn't understand how the world worked.

Geelong finished third last that season. We had to wait again.

Over the summer we had a lot of fun, catching yabbies in the creek, swimming at the pool and in the Goulburn River, making cubbyhouses. We were always riding around. We looked forward to Little Athletics at

Princes Park each Saturday morning. Peter, David and I were all pretty handy, although not world-beaters. We ran for the Red Devils club—Dad was the club secretary.

We practised all the events. Dad had made us high jump posts and we used a curtain rod as the bar. We even got to mind some of the official equipment during the week. We used the stop watches to do time trials: once around the block, twice around the block, once around the house. Peter and I discovered the discus. We worked out how to do the spin from reading a coaching manual and we improved quickly. It was all about timing. It was about feeling the forces coming together, your left hip clearing and your hand flinging out the discus along the tangent off your right hip.

We both won the local final and then, amazingly, won the regional final in our respective age groups. We had a chance to go to the state titles. Our event, however, was to be on a Sunday at Olympic Park. I was nearly ten but I had not once missed church on a Sunday. Sometimes I'd go with Dad out to Girgarre on a Sunday night as well. Dad wasn't too keen for us to go to the state championships but we were desperate to. Eventually we were allowed to make the decision for ourselves although when we said we were going it felt like we'd made the wrong decision. But weren't we developing our gifts? Clearly I was no Eric Liddell.

The weekend was a disaster. I felt very guilty as I stood waiting for my turn that Sunday morning at Olympic Park. As each Gulliver took his throw I sat there, the lone Lilliputian. The guy who won, Quigley, went on to throw the discus for Australia and is now making a living from the strongest-man-in-the-world circuit tossing cabers, pulling trains and lifting big round rocks.

It was coming into footy season and being in grade five I could try out for the school squad. I would also return to club footy and continue trying to get a game with Shepparton. School was good—I had a great teacher, Mr Murray, who was the school footy coach. He loved football. But he also loved schoolwork and reading.

Things were rolling along. It was a time when you had faith in life, that things were going to turn out the way you hoped; that in time you *would* play on the half forward flank for Shepparton, that algebra would not be the mystery you thought it would be, that school milk would not be the hurdle it always had been, that Geelong would fight back, that Larry Donohue would become a champion. That life would serve you well.

Not long into the year, however, Dad got a 'call' to Oakey in Queensland. He accepted. We were leaving Shepparton; leaving everything we'd worked towards; leaving football.

Even though we weren't to leave until the middle of the year I didn't bother signing on with Shepparton. I did try out for the school squad, though. I was on the verge of being selected. I know because Mr Murray told me. He called me aside after practice and explained that it was best for the team if he put in another grade five, one who could get some experience so that he'd be a better player the following year. I was devastated.

The squad trained on the main oval. I played house footy with the leftovers on the rectangular field next door. One day I kicked four goals playing at full forward. It wasn't too hard. My opponent, a rotund full back with his bum-crack showing at the top of his shorts, spent most of the time sitting in the goal square. I led out at one stage and could feel no breath nor hear any footsteps behind me. I stood under the wobbly kick and took an easy chest mark. I looked over to see my opponent sitting in the square picking out and eating yum-yum weed. I have never thought those goals counted.

During those games I would stand looking across to the other oval where the real footballers were. They were talked to as if they were footballers, they thought of themselves as footballers and maybe, had I played on the school team, I would have found a way of belonging with them.

I used to have great talks with Mr Murray. I think he liked me. I think he knew how I saw the world. He asked me to become the goal umpire for the school side so I got to be part of it all on Friday afternoons. I was a very earnest goal umpire.

Things were about to change. We kept following the footy as closely as ever—listening and watching and reading—until the time came for us to leave. Geelong kept losing, miserably.

We packed up our lives and prepared to start again.

CHAPTER 5

It is Saturday afternoon. We have lived in Oakey for three years or so. I have played my Under-13 rugby league match at the local footy ground. We've been thrashed again. I'm a bit sore and have a few tag marks. They'd be stop marks if I still lived in Victoria. I have that warm feeling of having done something that matters.

I eat my lunch. I try to get the VFL on Radio Australia but the reception on the radiogram is terrible. There are about three stations all in the one place. This sometimes happens on short-wave. Geelong is having another horrible season which worries me. But it also means that I'm not overly concerned when I can't find the coverage. I don't persevere. I'll get the progress scores on the ABC.

I read the newspaper for a while. I kick the footy for a while. I walk around the garden for a while, chipping a couple of golf balls. I go back inside for a while. Mum notices. 'Why don't you do your homework?' she asks. There's no way I'm doing my homework on a Saturday. Saturdays are for sport. I read my Ivan Southall novel for a while. That doesn't feel right either. It's Saturday.

I get on my bike and ride the few kilometres out to the Oakey Army Aviation Base by myself. I hope there's a game of real footy on. There is: Army Aviation are playing Coolaroo from Toowoomba. I sit on one of the forms by the fence. I rest my chin on my hands on the fence rail. It doesn't look much like footy on TV but it's not such a bad game. I am drawn into it. I join the army huddle at three-quarter time. Only a few of us stand around: the trainers, a few guys in uniform, a few servicemen who have come to watch their southern mates. They wonder who I am. I watch the last quarter. I can't remember who wins. I ride home.

What makes a boy ride some distance, by himself, to watch a game of very ordinary footy where neither of the teams means anything to him? What is he thinking? What does he imagine?

My mother sobbed as we drove out of Shepparton for the last time. I was worried about leaving the place that I knew; the place where I was comfortable. I was very worried about football. Everyone in Victoria said we were mad to leave. They said that people were so backward in Queensland that they couldn't spell beer and that rugby was a stupid game where you needed no skill—you could even throw the ball—and you were likely to be mortally wounded. We kept driving north and when the familiar four posts on green ovals gave way to funny looking H-shaped things near West Wyalong my understanding of the world was seriously challenged.

We arrived in Oakey in August 1972. The move was made easier by Geelong's abysmal form—we had lost the first nine games that year. The season had been written off. But Ian Chappell's Australians were doing well in England and the Munich Olympics were around the corner. We were so looking forward to the Games and, as young athletes, to the prospect of one day representing Australia ourselves.

Oakey is a small town just west of Toowoomba. It sits among the last hills before the vast fertile plain of the Darling Downs spreads out towards Roma. In those days it had about two thousand people.

Arriving for the first time, we drive down the main street—a long thoroughfare of houses, schools, pubs, a swimming pool, a railway station and a few old shops. It is as if no one is game to live more than a couple of blocks away from the main road. Peter, David and I sit wide-eyed in the back seat. What is this place? Mum is having serious doubts, I can tell. Dad stops the Vee-Dub outside the local primary school and explains tactically how much character it has. Like many Queensland buildings, it is on stilts, a classic colonial structure established in 1874. The expansive grounds include rugby fields, netball courts, tennis courts, palm trees, gum trees, pepper trees, and gardens. The grass is all brown, the colour frozen out of it by Oakey's frosty nights. There are no people around. 'You'll like it here, hey fellas?' Dad says in a voice part pastoral and part fatherly. I suspect the lads at Gowrie Street State School were right: we really have landed back in the early fifties.

Even so, we just got on with it. We had been taught from an early age to do our best so that each new challenge was tackled with a self-measuring sincerity. As was our family's way, we established new rhythms, and they were engaging enough. Every morning we sat on the steps on the front verandah eating toast and Vegemite. We listened to the ABC's cricket report from England which began with a song:

Here come the Aussies and cricket is our game
We're all together and winning is our aim
Oh we'll play on through the English rain
And win the Ashes back again

They nearly did. We cleaned our school shoes and read the local paper. The *Toowoomba Chronicle* described an alien world of farm machinery, grain prices and rugby league. Dad ordered the *Australian*. We had never heard of the national daily while in Victoria but it was better than the *Courier-Mail* which hid its token

VFL coverage somewhere around the trots form. We were among heathens.

The newsagent wouldn't deliver the *Australian* because it was just something he didn't do. So each morning one of us would ride down to the newsagent to pick it up. I'd usually go through the lane by the Grand Hotel and onto the main street. At 7.15 a.m. there wasn't much happening. Old Ned Ehrlich and his mates sat for their morning chat on the bench outside the Commonwealth Bank opposite the war memorial. The publican at the Western Line hosed down his foot-path. A semitrailer would break the morning quiet.

On Tuesday afternoons I'd go down and get our specially ordered copy of Monday's Melbourne *Sun*. This was the week's highlight even though the Cats were going from bad to worse. I devoured all the match reports to see what was really happening down there.

Despite the changes we were accepting of life in Oakey. Dad's work had purpose. He had come to tend the Lutheran flock which consisted of three congregations: one in Oakey, and two among the wheat and sorghum at Aubigny and Norwin. About six hundred Lutherans had lived in the district for years. They were easy to pick with names like Ziebell, Bothmann, Hausler, Nuske, Ciesiolka, Folker, Schelberg and so on. They had come as German peasants in the late nineteenth century. Their hard work had seen them prosper and now some of them were wealthy land-owners with huge plants of equipment and dams and tax problems. Others struggled.

All I knew was that somehow we had to make our way. On the first school morning we polished our black shoes and dressed in our old uniforms and went off to be enrolled. Peter and I landed in Mr Crameri's grade four/five composite class. We'd never heard of having two grades in one room. We were presented to the class: two skinny little kids from Victoria wearing grey shirts instead of blue. As I looked around, I forgot how nervous I was. The desks still had inkwells (unused of course), and the swirly writing on the blackboard looked like it came out of a nineteenth-century copy-book. We used a sort of running printing in Shepparton. The girls wore what could only be described as bloomers under their dresses—grandma bike-pants in heavy cotton in the school colours of blue with a yellow trim. Some of the boys had World War II haircuts—short back and sides with the sides really shaved. They had big ears and big Adam's apples and they grinned. Quite a few were barefoot even though it was still winter. A row of hats lined the wall like a museum exhibition—old Depression-style hats that your grandpa might wear when he went to town or to a funeral. They didn't have school bags, they had ports, which were kept on the port racks.

To begin, Mr Crameri said, 'Sit up straight,' which elicited the most remarkable response. Chairs were straightened and those in them sat with ramrod spines which actually arched backwards. They folded their arms across their puffed chests. All of these movements filled the room with noise for a few seconds. Mr Crameri's warm introduction coincided with the need of the entire class to draw breath, and slowly spines relaxed, arms went limp, and normal breathing patterns resumed. These people were a bit different, but I didn't care. I had to become one of them. I was, however, a little concerned whether I was going to be able to.

At 'little lunch' the schoolyard pecking order became clear. For a start, girls and boys remained separate. Among the boys Noel Leahy, a little snowy-haired fellow with skin so fair it was almost translucent, was the ringleader. There was no doubt about that. He strolled around like Muhammad Ali with most of the other boys—the sons of old Oakey—trailing him like an entourage of henchmen. Noel's parents owned the Commercial Hotel. This carried considerable weight with his henchmen. But he had his own qualities. He was a sportsman: he could whip the whole grade over a hundred metres, he could jump, and he could play rugby league.

Rather than joining the entourage for the break, I sat on one of the logs and ate my Saladas. Clearly, I was odd. But it seemed to bamboozle some of them. Stephen Hedge came over to me in his official capacity as ambassador for Noel Leahy and spat, 'Can yuh run?'

Could I run? I reckoned I could run. I was a sportsman from Victoria. I thought of myself as a player, a follower and an admirer of sport. How many of Leahy's henchmen kept scrapbooks? How many of them watched golf on TV? How many of them could name the jumper number of most VFL players? How many of them understood the evil that dwelt in the Collingwood Football Club? How many of them had been to the test cricket or were listening to the radio coverage of the tests in England at that very time? I was carving out parallel careers in football, cricket and athletics. I owed it to myself to reply as I did: 'Oh yeah, I can run.'

Hedge assumed the superior position, 'You couldn't beat Tosh.' Tosh was Noel Leahy's middle name. Those who knew him well called him Tosh.

'I'll race him if you like,' I offered.

Hedge looked at me like I was an idiot.

A course was mapped out; a distance of about sixty metres. We took off our shoes and the race was on. I felt confident but hadn't for one second considered the consequences of losing—or indeed, winning. I just did the best I could. In fact I tried my heart out.

Stride for stride, we crossed the line together. It was a God-given dead heat and everyone was willing to say it was. Leahy's entourage looked stunned and for a moment I wondered what was going to happen. There was a pause and then Noel came over, put his arm around my shoulders and we walked back to our shoes. 'You're going to make a great five eighth,' he said.

'What's that?' I asked.

'The position outside the half back,' Noel explained.

'Yeah,' a voice chimed in from the pack, 'and Tosh is the half back.'

I wanted to explain that I was actually going to make a top-class rover, but I'd have been wasting my breath.

I had to wait until the following autumn to become part of the Oakey Junior Rugby League Football Club, the Oakey Bears. I didn't realise how important the sign-on ritual was, and my absence didn't go unnoticed. Everyone at school knew I was intending to play. I wanted to play rugby league because that's what you did if you were a boy in Oakey. I was going to be an Oakey Bear because already I felt like an Oakey Bear, even if I was an Oakey Bear who kept a VFL scrapbook and had a Geelong pennant on my wall.

The fact that I knew nothing about rugby league seemed no more than a minor problem. It was a game I didn't understand. What was the purpose of those scrums? How could you possibly run straight at someone knowing you were going to get pummelled? In real footy you tried to keep away from the tacklers. I was, however, getting an idea of rugby league from watching the ABC replays of Brisbane matches and from watching the local A-grade matches, but I still had a long way to go.

So too, it became obvious, did many of my team-mates. As Under-12s we were one of the worst teams ever to strap on footy boots. (I had high-cut Duncan Halls.) Not only were we a small side physically, we had few skills to speak of. Tosh was the exception.

Looking back now, the coach also had no skills to speak of. He was a clerk at the local shire council and was from out of town. His appointment as the Under-12 coach had all the hallmarks of an evening on the grog at the Western Line. It was possible that some official from the OJRL, desperate to find coaches, challenged him to pass on the skills he professed to have to the youth of the district.

He was a terrible coach. There were times when he didn't even turn up to training. When he did he made us run, and run, and run. We spent two full seasons running up and down passing the ball to each other. The training ground at Oakey was like a frozen tundra: night after night of frost had left it rock solid. You didn't want to fall over on it. You certainly didn't want to bang your head on it. We weren't even that keen to run on it. But sessions would finish with laps run in single file where the last person sprinted around to the front of the line. Some of our players took three-quarters of a lap to grind their way to the front even though the leader had almost stopped to a walk. Running and more running. We all suffered from shin splints.

Oakey winters were severe. By the end of footy training you could feel the frost descending. You could feel the cold in your chest and in your mouth. Your nose hurt. Your feet froze. When you got home you'd be too cold to get into the bath, it would hurt too much. You'd wake up the next morning and it would be minus six degrees. Oakey would be on the ABC weather. We competed with Stanthorpe for the state's minimum. You didn't want to get out of bed. You certainly needed gloves to ride to school. But, when there was a frost in the morning, you knew that it would be one of those cloudless Queensland winter days where, if you could get away from any wind, you could enjoy the sun's warmth.

On occasions our coach would try to explain some skill to us—perhaps a tackling technique or something about drawing the man—but he had trouble keeping our attention. It was more likely that Mudguts Hudson, our rotund prop (who would have been standing in the goal square at full back had he grown up in Victoria), and Stephen Hedge would be 'wrasslin' on the ground. Sadly, they showed little of this energy or aggression on the field on Saturdays. There were times when I thought Noel was going to just do his block, 'What are you blokes doin' here? Why do you even bother coming to training? Just shut up and listen.' He didn't though. It was what I was thinking as well—but I didn't think it was my place to speak.

The boys weren't too fired up about being world beaters at football. In fact they didn't care if we didn't beat anyone. They were there because it was what you did if you were an Oakey boy. And the bus trips to Toowoomba and places like Pittsworth and Gatton were a lot of fun. They could buy pies, bubble gum and soft drink and play up in the bus. It was not uncommon to receive a dead arm or worse, a dead leg, from someone up the back of the bus—on the way to football. And they were team-mates. Oakey mothers were happy to finance their own little bit of Saturday peace. But to expect the sons of old Oakey to think the raison d'etre of such trips was success at football was asking a bit too much.

I started out playing at full back because I could catch and I could kick. I continued to call catching 'marking'. It was impossible for me to lose this language. When we kicked the footy around at training I didn't drop a chest mark. No one in Victoria beyond the age of eight and a half dropped an uncontested chest mark. It didn't matter how high or long the kick, I could get under it and mark it. It was no big deal. At Oakey, however, it stood out. My reputation was confirmed at the Athletic Oval at an Oakey versus Newtown A-grade game when I was sitting on the side-line with a few of the lads. When the Newtown bloke kicked for touch, I jumped up, stood under the wobbling fifty-yard bomb, and marked the ball half on my chest and half on my face. The footy was nearly as big as me and all the adults around felt obliged to comment, 'Wow. Great catch, mate.' 'Good on yuh, mate.' 'Jeez, you're a gutsy little bastard.' I sat down with a fat lip—one of those ones the size of a scorched almond that comes up instantly. (These were the days when the fat lip was a common childhood ailment; days when kids got warts rather than asthma and chilblains rather than ADD.)

When we got a penalty I got to kick for touch. I was the only kid on the Darling Downs kicking in the style of Peter McKenna. They had never seen a drop punt before. Most kids kicked like rugby league players—a hook-footed torpedo which only got distance if it spun properly. As a scrawny kid with insect legs, I relied on timing to propel the footy any distance. Even then the footy wouldn't go very far, but my kicks were pretty accurate.

I was still apprehensive about the physical demands of football. Rugby league was even more about the clash of bodies than real footy. The difference here was that you knew when the clashes were coming. I was scared of tackling. I also lacked the natural technique and tackling was something we hardly ever practised. The ground was too hard. I just knew it would really, really hurt.

I was happy to be kept at full back where I didn't have to tackle as much. Our defensive line was never secure, though, and I had to at least get my body in the way of plenty of opposing players. One day I found myself chasing a kid who was about my pace. He was going flat out and I was no more than a metre behind him. All I needed to do was throw myself at him. We ran over the half-way line. I could hear the screams from the supporters on the sideline: 'Dive. Dive. Dive.' I knew that's what I had to do. But I couldn't do it. I could hear my own voices: 'You can't do that; you might hurt yourself.' We got to the twenty-five. I followed him. I'm not sure whether I was going full pace. He put the ball over the try-line. For most of the run I could have reached out and touched him. I was embarrassed as I walked back to the half-way line.

I was that gutless Victorian kid who could catch and kick. Later that season I was presented with an opportunity to redeem myself. Suddenly from just wandering around at full back, half concentrating on the game, I found myself in the action. It happened in the slow–fast way of an accident. A huge Souths forward had burst through and was bolting towards me. This was a test. He was twice my size: a sort of superhuman juggernaut in shoulder pads. I showed him the sideline like they did on TV and as he went to go around me I accelerated into him. I felt my shoulder find its place on his thigh and I drove with my legs and I barrelled him into touch. It was one of those moments, those quirks of timing, when the cosmic forces have come together to your advantage. It was like being in a wave at Burleigh Heads. It was like one of those moments in golf where your driver goes that extra thirty metres. We were both off the ground. We both landed over near the fence, me on top. I was as shocked as anyone, including the Souths bloke who got up nursing a sore bum (because that's what it was called by this stage) and a damaged ego. That had never happened to him before at Oakey. I jogged back to my position thinking, 'Jeepers. Where did that come from?' All the parents and supporters cheered. I remember the wonder in their voices, 'Good tackle mate.' 'Good on yuh son.' I felt lifted; alert to the game. I could do it, and it didn't even hurt. Not that the tackle helped much. We lost the game. In fact we lost every game that season.

But we still kept turning up.

CHAPTER 6

I missed Geelong. We followed them in the newspapers, but it was difficult. We were exiles in a footy wilderness. No one talked about footy. No one knew how good it was; how it made you feel. No one knew how much one person could love a football club. It was all very private. I was suffering in silence—the Cats had another crook season which started miserably and got worse. We finished second last.

When I arrived in Oakey I decided to pick some rugby league teams to barrack for. Rather than go with the winners I chose the sides on the bottom of the premiership tables: in Brisbane I chose perennial battlers Wynnum Manly and in Sydney I chose Wests who were near the bottom and wore Oakey colours. In the English soccer I chose the bottom club in the fourth division, Doncaster Rovers, although I had a soft spot for West Ham and Billy Bond who were often on Brian Moore's 'Match of the Day'. I was allowed to stay up to watch the English soccer which I started to follow quite keenly. I loved listening to BBC 'Sports Round-up' late on Sunday afternoons with its familiar music and that brilliant voice. 'But first the football results. English First Division: Arsenal nil, Wolverhampton Wanderers nil; Aston Villa 1, West Bromwich Albion nil; Chelsea 3, Liverpool 2; Derby County 1, Leeds 1,' all the way to the fourth division, 'Scunthorpe 2, Halifax 4.' I would wait for Doncaster and be pleased or disappointed according to the result and would look forward to seeing the results in print and looking at the tables in the *Australian* on Monday mornings. I much preferred Brian Moore to Jimmy Hill who looked like Lancelot in the King Arthur cartoon.

The QRL games from Brisbane could be exciting. I got to know the players: blokes like Nev Hornery whom I liked because he was always potting field goals, Hughie O'Doherty and Ross Strudwick at Valleys, Ian Dauth and his funny kicking style, and Bunny Pearce from Redcliffe. I also followed the local Toowoomba games often broadcast by the excitable Pat O'Shea. As I lay on my bed and listened I could see the players and the backline moves. 'It comes from McKeiver at dummy half, to Millett, to Rose; Rose looks to Arnold; he throws the dummy and cuts back inside. He's through. Rose is in the clear. He comes to Platz. He looks outside, and finds Muirhead, back to Rose and Rose'll score. He's over. He's over under the posts. Dicky Rose, you are a genius. Dicky Rose has put it down, right underneath the black dot and the Bears are right back in this. Wattles 18, Oakey 13 with the kick to come.'

I had seen the boys play at Oakey and it was easy to picture this happening because I hardly missed a Sunday game. This was typical country football, just like in Shepparton, with tooting cars and nervous mums with thermoses and sandwiches, and dads sitting on the fold-up chair in front of the dusty Ford having a quiet beer. They all squinted into the western sun. A couple of blokes in aprons walked along selling 'Doubles on the main game.'

The real drinkers stood on the other side of the ground, between the canteen, the bar and the dunnies (you couldn't call them toilets). The licensed area was fenced off by a series of star pickets joined by rope. Inside the drinking pen blokes had immunity from prosecution for bad language, despite the proximity of women, children and touch judges. It was the sort of place where meatworkers and farmhands could fart freely (and get a laugh for it) and give advice of similar substance to players, coaches and especially referees. They chanted, 'Get 'em on-side' when the opposition encroached within the five metres and 'Don't ask the linesman, ask y'guide dog you deadshit, Barrett.'

Oakey had an outstanding senior team which meant that somewhere after the Under-12s and before the A-grade there was quantum improvement. Or possibly another explanation: Oakey were first-class recruiters. They were far better at it than Geelong, who were struggling to find anyone who could help them up the ladder. The Oakey scouts looked west and they found plenty of big blokes.

During the '73 season I was sometimes a sand boy. This was a great honour but to make the start of the Under-16s I had to leave church as soon as the Benediction finished, which meant I'd miss the last hymn. I didn't have time to change. The footy field was two hundres metres away from the church so I'd sprint out the church door, over the road, across the railway line, and make it just in time. I was probably the only sand boy to carry out his duties wearing deep purple flares, a matching purple jumper with a white panel on the front and my Sunday shoes. I wore this clobber every week to church and every week to football for the entire season.

The next year I preferred to sit in the little wooden grandstand. I made a conscious decision to take up this vantage point because it was where Leanne and Margi Evans sat when they came to the football.

There were few things better than watching the Oakey reserve grade knowing that the Evans sisters were around. Leanne was every bit as lovable as Chrissy from 'Man about the House'. I fantasised about her spotting me in the grandstand; I imagined that her eyes would light up, she'd waltz straight up to me, sit down and put her head on my shoulder while Oakey marched triumphantly to victory in the A-grade.

She never did. I don't remember having a proper conversation with her at the football. But there is no doubt that you could count the seconds when I didn't know precisely where she was. When I noticed she was buying something at the canteen I would race down and stand next to her as if the chance collision of our appetitic orbits actually meant something. 'G'day Evans,' was all I would say but I wanted her to know that there was so much more in my heart. I wanted her to know about Geelong and VFL Park and my scrapbooks. I wanted to show her our family photos.

The smell of the pies would bring me back to reality. They were locally made and had gravy and flaky pastry. Fat women in aprons would cut the top off so they could add a huge spoonful of mushy peas which gurgled away in the saucepan like hot mud in Rotorua. Sometimes I'd have a hot dog. A thick saveloy with half the skin off would be plucked from the cauldron of bubbling red liquid, to be placed sloppily on an unevenly buttered bread roll with tomato sauce. Butter was always unspreadable during Oakey winters.

When the westerlies blew the grandstand offered little protection from the chill. The wind forced its way through the gaps between the wooden boards and it was hard to keep warm. Old ladies in tartan skirts with safety pins and cameo brooches clapped happily as they struggled to keep the blanket over their legs. Their coat-and-tie husbands showed the restraint of their station but when Oakey scored one of their scintillating tries there was just enough smirk on their faces to indicate they were as excited as young boys again. When you were battling to keep your pie from toppling they looked at you and your happy, messy face and winked. They knew.

It was warmer when we cheered; when we were drawn into the drama of the game. I really did want Oakey to win. They were our boys. This was our town. We had great forwards like Peter Connell, who was as tough a footballer as you'd find and loved a blue. He wore a guard on his forearm and legend had it around Oakey Primary that it concealed an iron rod. Connell was a tackling machine and could bust through the middle of the ruck. Sel Murphy came from Tara. He was a giant with carrot orange hair, and his rosy cheeks made him look too harmless to play prop. Occasionally something would light his fuse, as if someone had insulted his mother or his sister, or stolen his rosary beads, and his gentleness would give way to the sort of fire written about in ancient myths. For a few minutes the game would be his. And then he would be left exhausted and standing doubled over with the hooker, Lex McKeiver, as they waited for the next scrum. 'Push, Oakey. Push.'

It was the backs I most remember. It was impossible

to conceive of a better backline in the rugby league playing world. I have a strong image of them in my mind. They are lined out on the Oakey ground. The light has lost its whiteness and has turned the gold of a late winter's afternoon. A scrum is packed on the twenty-five near the far touchline and the Oakey backline is set so that the open winger is standing at the twenty-five at the other end of the field. What a sight! When they win the ball they run it at full pace and with faultless precision. Spike Weimers is at half back. Dicky Rose is at five eighth. He is an Aboriginal player with long skinny legs which look like they'd snap if he were tackled, and a skinny waist and then on top of this dodgy foundation, a big chest. He is a handsome sort of bloke with a cheeky smile. It is also a reassuring smile; a smile that lets you know that he is in concert with the football gods. More often than not it is Dicky Rose's sheer brilliance which gets us out of trouble. I love him. We all love him.

The inside centre is Terry Arnold, another bloke from way out west. His ancient jockstrap hangs outside the back of his shorts. He has good hands. His partner is Nev Tate who doesn't say much. He's just quick. On the wing is one of the crowd's favourites, Willy Weatherall, who has the sort of talent that leaves you shaking your head, saying, 'Can you believe that?' He turns slim chances into tries and makes you punch the arm of the person next to you in delight. You have little control over these responses. At full back is Mal

Muirhead, a specialist at chiming into the backline. He is so good at it that at little lunches under the pepper tree we argue whether passes have been intended for him or whether he has run onto passes directed at Arnold and Tate. Oakey wins the scrum and the ball comes through the hands and when Weatherall gets it he's going like Hasely Crawford only quicker, and he dives at the corner and there are bodies and a corner post and a chubby touch judge and the flag stays down and it's a try. In one match Oakey beat Valleys 61–0. For a joke they let McKeiver take a shot at goal. We like Lex McKeiver because he's a veteran. He's Cassie's dad and she's in our class.

At about the same time the A-grade was thrashing Valleys, we were getting hammered by their Under-12s. There was no doubt we were an ordinary side but the preparation for that match was less than ideal. With five minutes to go before we were to run on that day at Valleys, there were only nine of us togged up; the rest were over nicking carrots from the market garden on Pillar Street.

I liked togging up: that moment standing bare-chested in the winter cold pulling on a jumper that was so big there was too much to tuck into your shorts. We wore black jumpers with a white V. At Oakey we got dressed in the home dressing room, a dungeon-like recess under the grandstand. We'd put our boots on and then go outside and pass the ball around while our coach offered advice. It was never specific advice.

There were never strategies. It was always 'Do your best boys,' and an occasional 'Do it for Oakey.' The problem was we didn't know *what* to do. As we ran out we looked like we were wearing the Under-15s' jumpers.

We were hopeful—but only in the sense that that's what we were supposed to be. I liked the expectant nervousness before the game; the same feeling you had before you did a lecturette at school. We were a team which ran out expecting to play—but never expecting to win. We couldn't afford to make winning too important otherwise we'd have begun to exhibit the early signs of clinical depression. It was already bad enough for me—I was a Geelong supporter.

One day at Newtown we started brilliantly. We took the ball from the kick off and held it for six tackles. Then Hector Varley won the first scrum and a couple of forwards rucked it up before Tosh called out, 'Backs' ball.' He took the pass from Varley, dummied to me, ran through a hole, stepped the full back and ran fifty metres to score under the posts. He converted his own try and we led 5–0. Back at half way it was as if we'd won the premiership. It was the first time we'd ever led in a game and one of the few times we'd ever scored. We lost 40–5.

By this time I had moved in to five eighth. Tosh had been right. I liked the responsibility that playing five eighth brought. 'Move up, Oakey,' I'd say to encourage the backs to come up in a single defensive line; 'Centre a side,' when scrums were formed in the middle of the park. Sometimes I'd get it wrong and Tosh would correct me. In one match against All Whites I threw three passes in a row that were intercepted by my opposite number. Even Tosh was annoyed with me that day: 'If he's coming up that quick just run through the gap. You have to be able to get in behind him.' I had little idea of what he was talking about.

We went through another season without a win— without coming close to a win. In one match at Oakey our local referee Mr Costello started helping us out on the field. He was a nice bloke. He had three daughters and had turned to refereeing in the absence of foot-balling progeny. Bearing a remarkable resemblance to Foghorn Leghorn, he wore the same gear that the refs' association had given him years before and it was old, faded and uncomfortably tight. His protruding belly created a substantial sway and this put such pressure on his legs that his knees wobbled in all directions. Either he felt sorry for us or he was getting frustrated watching us. By some miracle during one match we had forced our way to within ten yards of the try-line. A scrum was packed and Mr Costello gave us a penalty. As Mr Costello faced us with his arm outstretched he whispered from the corner of his mouth, 'Take the tap and go the blind.' We did. But we didn't get over for a try.

Our best season was definitely Under-13. While kids all over the Darling Downs had grown over that summer, we remained the same short, skinny lot we'd always been. At the start of that year Millmerran produced their secret new weapon—a farmboy called David Uebergang. He was huge. We called him David Choobergang. He was kind of flabby but with plenty of muscle underneath. I remember laughing while watching five of our fleas cling to bits of him and his maroon jumper as he carried them all down field. I would have jumped on too but there was nowhere to grab.

We did a lot of tackling and we needed sound technique to get the bigger kids down. We had to tackle low and fall with their weight. They didn't scare us anymore. Without even noticing I had overcome the fear that football might hurt me. I just played—and tackled and tackled and tackled. Often the relentless surge saw the floodgates open. We hardly ever had the footy—just getting possession was cause for celebration although we weren't so adept at using it.

We still had the same coach. He got us to practise the same move every week at training. The forwards would pack a scrum near the touch line. The backs would be lined out. I'd stand a little wider than usual. Varley would yell 'Won black' and the ball would trickle out between Rynnie's legs. The forwards would stumble forward and tumble over like the Keystone Cops. Noel would pick up the ball and the blind winger would make the extra man between Noel and me. He'd pass it to me and it would go through the hands along the backline. The open winger would sprint up field and we'd back up until the coach blew the whistle. The forwards would jog over, wait for Mudguts, and pack another scrum and we'd repeat the move. In four years of fixtures we never once used the move.

I used to stand there watching Patty Sexton coaching the Under-16s on the next field. He made sense. There was discipline. They did drills and practised simple but important things like keeping the defensive line straight—up and back and up and back. He took us for training once. He showed us how to put a player through a gap; how to structure an attack for six tackles. Mr Jones coached the Under-15s. He was really keen and had a helper who kept stats. How I wanted a coach who would sit us down on Tuesday night and tell us how many tackles we'd made on Saturday like Mr Jones did. But we just kept jogging, and making sure the blind winger knew when to join the line.

We were presented with an opportunity early that season. Allora–Clifton produced junior sides of similar skill to Oakey. I never looked at a premiership table to see how we were going because all we needed to know was that if we could beat Clifton we wouldn't finish bottom.

I remember the match against Allora–Clifton at Oakey in 1975 clearly because it was the *only* match we won in four years of junior footy. My brother Peter plays on the wing. I play five eighth, as always. Mum and Dad come to watch, which is rare. It is an unusually muggy morning for Oakey and during the game the heavens open. A torrential downpour leaves ankle-deep water in the low-lying areas of the uneven field. One of our players loses a boot in a puddle and about four of us swish our hands around in it before it is discovered. The score is 5–5 for a long time but Clifton is getting on top. Tosh appeals to us all and we defend grimly. We manage to find some inner reserve—for once there is real hope. The conditions are absurd. Water splashes everywhere. The ball is like a peeled mango. Somehow we wind up with it and make a break down the field. We have players to the left of the play-the-ball. Tosh calls, 'Backs' ball' and runs across field and links up with me. The defenders slip over. I send it straight on. There is a chain of passes; more than we've ever completed on the driest of days. The ball gets to Vohland in the centres who passes it to our illustrious prop Mudguts Hudson, who accepts the pass, runs a few metres and falls over the line. Try. We can't believe it. Mudguts gets up like it's stock-standard. He is a hero. We win 8–5. We dance off. Jubilant. Sodden. For a whole week we are footballers. Clearly, we are good in the wet.

Later that season we ventured to Clifton for the return match. Although there wasn't a cloud in the sky we were confident. But Clifton skipped away and we were unlikely to come back. We never came back. Frustration gave way to rising anger and anger sought release. One of our forwards knuckled one of the Clifton blokes and it triggered a reaction—in us. Even Tosh was using the swinging arm in tackles. I had never done anything mean or nasty on the footy field. If I accidentally stood on an opponent's hand or bumped into him while we were both watching the play I'd apologise.

This day, though, I found myself gritting my teeth and swinging my arm. I was wild with the disappointment of trailing the worst side. A Clifton player was being tackled when I came right over the top and swung my arm into his face. It was a well-timed Peter Connell forearm which smashed across his nose and mouth. In reality it was probably like being punched by Frank Spencer. These were the Countdown years and we were more Sherbert than Alice Cooper; more Leo Sayer than Bryan Ferry. Still, throwing the stiff arm felt good. The ref blew his whistle, loud. I tried to sneak away like a guilty dog. The ref yelled, 'Come 'ere Six.' He gave me a stern warning.

A few tackles later and Tosh and I went high again, both straight at the head of our opponent. The ref blew even harder. He walked away and shook his head in a vain attempt to foster guilt and repentance. There was little chance of that. 'Come 'ere Six, and you better come over as well, Seven.' He preached hard and told me I was lucky to stay on the field and that the next time we would both get an early shower. Not long after this the hooter sounded. We had been beaten. We had the hearts of those who have failed their consciences.

Everyone was angry in the dressing shed. A dozen feeble excuses rationalised our inadequacy; not one of them implicated us. When we got on the bus for the return trip to Oakey the driver sensed the mood. We giants of Oakey Junior Rugby League were hanging out the window giving the environs of greater Clifton the forks and yelling. 'Pack of fuckin' cheats,' 'Youse can all get fucked.' This went on until someone dropped one of their boots out the window. To his credit the driver ignored the appeals to stop.

I was disturbed at how easily all of this had happened. It was not the brutality: we were about as tough as Geelong. It was the wilfulness, the abandoning of any respect for our opponent, the gracelessness of it all. I have had the same feeling a number of times since. I felt it in the first quarter of the 1989 VFL grand final.

The following season, Under-14s, went by without a win although we were quite competitive on occasions. We had a couple of good games against Millmerran; one where we lost 24–16. But we remained the worst side in the club, the competition, and perhaps all of rugby league, and we were being made to look even more awful by the success of some of the younger Oakey teams who had the Teevan boys. Rohan and Craig went on to play NSWRL footy for various clubs.

We remained physically small. At the start of the Under-15 season when, at last, we got Mr Jones as our coach I was still only about forty kilograms (just over six stone). Tosh was about the same size. Not long after, he became an apprentice jockey. For every game I still wore the same jocks I'd had since grade seven— disgusting nylon leopard-skin ones. I called them my lucky jocks. It was only years later when recounting my junior footy career at a dinner party that someone pointed out they weren't lucky at all. One win in four years: I hadn't thought of that.

By then we were in grade ten. School football in Queensland was organised on the basis of weight. There were three divisions: a seven stone, a nine stone and the opens. In that grade ten year half of our club side could still play in the seven stone competition at school. No one could get near us. We threw the ball all over the place. We won the final against Crows Nest 21–0. Maybe we hadn't been that bad after all. We were just small.

At club level, however, we were playing against blokes nearly twice our weight who shaved and called for the ball in deep voices. Some wore jockstraps. When I was put onto the next planet by Pittsworth's Brett Kowitz the writing was on the wall. It was time to hang up the Gola boots.

CHAPTER 7

Rugby league had been a lot of fun, despite all the losses. Although I no longer played I still followed the Oakey Bears. When I wasn't at golf on Sunday afternoons I would lie on the bed doing my trigonometry homework or reading *Romeo and Juliet* or writing a history assignment on the Renaissance while listening to Pat O'Shea's call of the Toowoomba Rugby League on 4GR. I wanted Oakey to win.

But I had real footy in my heart. Shepparton seemed a lifetime away, but neither time nor distance could diminish my passion for Geelong and the VFL. Through all my years of playing rugby league and following the Oakey Bears I never forgot the Cats. They were always with me, and I was with them. It was a test of loyalty but I loved Geelong so much that I was never going to be seduced by anything else. Throughout the 1970s I felt like I kept up my side of the bargain but I'm not sure the Geelong Football Club did. They were tough times.

I continued to keep scrapbooks. Geelong finished sixth in 1974, two and a half games out of the five. That season's scrapbook finishes when the Geelong reserves are beaten in the preliminary final by Footscray. The cuttings from the grand final are included—but they have never been Clagged in.

There are a couple of pages for each round: the VFL match details, the article on the Geelong game, some photographs and the reserves ladder in my own handwriting which I calculated myself. Some of the cuttings are from the *Sun*, some from the *Australian*, and some are in the memorable pink of the *Sporting Globe*.

The round four pages include an article by Scot Palmer about the Cats' dismal loss to St Kilda, in which Michael Turner made an eyecatching debut. It begins, 'Geelong is a football club far different from the rest. Its people have the unique ability of smiling when all that surrounds them is sorrow. From out of the black and murky abyss they will find something bright and shiny that will gladden their hearts and keep them happy till next time.' How was an eleven-year-old supposed to react to this? It was alarming for a kid to have his worst suspicions confirmed by an adult writing in the nation's premier football daily.

I was committed to Geelong but sometimes it felt like too much of a burden. The 1975 scrapbook starts out enthusiastically. There is some design flair: jagged-edged headlines across photos, paragraphs cut out, a goal-kicking tally at the front. But Geelong started poorly. In round eight when Hawthorn beat us 17.11.113 to 5.10.40 to leave us 1–7, it was too much. The book goes no further. Geelong finished second last that year.

Things upset me. Why was it that Geelong could play so poorly against lowly sides and then come out and beat the team on top of the ladder? Why was it that when Geelong was four goals ahead at three-quarter time we were more likely to lose than when we were two goals behind? And the big one: how could Doug Wade go across to North Melbourne? Dad said North Melbourne was buying a premiership. They had Barassi.

I'd still try to get the footy on our Ming dynasty radiogram. I'd tune in around 1.45 and eventually find the VFL broadcast. Geelong games were rarely covered but I'd wait for a goal so that the commentators would go around the grounds and I'd write down all six scores. I'd have a preferred result in each fixture. There was a hierarchy of preference. One: Geelong thrashes their opponent. Two: Collingwood loses. Three: Hawthorn loses. Four: the club immediately above Geelong on the ladder loses by heaps so their percentage goes down. Five: all clubs above Geelong lose unless a top club is playing a club just above

Geelong. As the afternoon unfolds I would construct the ladder in my head.

Sometimes the signal would come through loud and clear and just when you thought you were in for a pleasant afternoon it would fade and would be consumed by Indonesian music. Doug Bigelow's voice would be drowned out by *wang-nung-tung-yung-cha-ping-dong* and you'd sit having your cultural parameters expanded while hoping the footy would come back. Sometimes an electronic screech would take over: a sort of tremulating undertone with machine gun static over the top. You'd just have to turn it down and, if it persisted, right off. Sometimes the footy reception would be perfect and just when you thought you were in for a happy afternoon the Radio Australia studio would break in: 'And now we cross to Redfern for this afternoon's big game: South Sydney versus St George.' Why did this always happen? Why were we never able to do something we wanted to do without interruption, interference, upset? It was so infuriating. I'd take my little red trannie outside and listen to the QRL match from Brisbane and wait for the three-quarter-time scores. Sometimes it was ages after the game before we knew the final Geelong score. I'd mow the greens we had made and hit a few putts and go up the back of the fire station allotment and hit a few nine irons back into our yard.

Even though Geelong struggled through much of the seventies I would stay up on Sunday night to watch the VFL's footy replay. 'The Winners' was like a letter from home. It was like a little package of fruit cake and chocolate and woollen socks sent to the front. It started around midnight and was hosted by Drew Morphett or Peter Gee and included fifteen minutes of play from three games, as well as a summary of the round, the ladder and a few of the better marks and goals. I lived for it. If Geelong was on it was even better. And if they won it was bliss.

Picture the scene: it's 12.45 a.m. School tomorrow. The frost has settled outside. It's about two degrees below. You sit underneath a blanket in front of a fan heater. You still feel cold. You were tired at ten o'clock but you haven't gone to bed. You watch your team lose to South Melbourne. It's a game they should have won. You hate it because the Cats are losing, but you still love it because it's footy. 'The Winners' finishes at half past one and now you're wide awake. You go to bed thinking about how the Cats can make the five. You read and re-read the fixture list. You tell yourself that one day it will be easier.

We played kick-to-kick a lot after school. Sometimes we'd finish with a game of touch with a few of our mates but we always started with kick-to-kick. We had a proper Australian football—not a rugby league ball— even if it was an imitation Match II, made in Pakistan. It was a dodgy brand but it actually had a bit of symmetry. You could make a torp fly, and the drop punt was no problem. But it didn't have the perfect balance and weight and shape of a top footy. Peter and I kicked for ages, often without any chat, and with little movement. You'd kick and watch the slow end-over-end flight of the drop punt. Peter would mark it on his chest. He'd kick and you'd take a safe overhead mark. You'd get onto a drop kick and delight in its piercing parabolic path. He'd kick a torp back. Kick. Mark. Kick. Mark.

It was good when David came out. We'd take it in turns at contesting marks only David was a terrible kick so he rarely put the ball in the right place for us. I loved that feeling of flying with someone, the way that when you were in a bit of form you could let the contact propel you to where you needed to be to take the mark. I loved it when Peter set it up for the speccie and you'd stick your knee in David's back and get the real ride. This was one of the great feelings in sport; in life. You could feel that pause and that force that helped you, and you just knew when one had come off because David would sprawl forward and Peter would go, 'Ah, yeah.' Peter was a mollydooker. He kicked torps which bent like Max Walker's in-swingers. He'd get onto one and it would go over your head and you'd run back and just put out one hand and it would stick. I loved how footies were unpredictable, how they bounced like fingerprints. I loved the feel of them, the smell of them. I decided that when I went to uni I was definitely going to play footy. I wanted to play in a game. I wanted to come flying past on the wing like Micky Turner and burst clear and send a thirty-metre handball to some team-mate on the run.

We saw Micky Turner in round seven in 1978. We were in Melbourne for the May holidays and we went to Waverley. It was the first time we'd seen Geelong in seven years. Melbourne finished bottom that season, but that in no way prevented them from putting in a big one against us that day. They jumped us. Greg Wells and Robbie Flower kept setting up at half back, without their Geelong opponents. They rushed through the square at each centre bounce and kept getting the ball on the fly. It was terrible. Why weren't the Geelong guys picking them up? They led by eight goals at three-quarter time. We'd scored a miserable nine by then. After that we got going. We got a few early ones and then we just ran everywhere. It had been cold and wet all day but we were warm with the prospect of a miraculous win. Melbourne steadied and won by a couple of goals. I still hadn't seen Geelong win.

Waverley was every bit as good as I thought it would be. People still wore the colours, they were still excited by their boys running through the banner, they still loved the first siren and the first ball-up, they still yelled at the umpires, they still told you what they thought of Geelong supporters. This time, though, it was a lot less threatening than when I'd gone to Victoria Park all those years before.

Being in Victoria for a couple of weeks made me realise how frustrating it was to follow footy from Oakey. It made me realise that Melbourne was footy. It was everywhere. Maybe one day I'd move to Melbourne; Geelong even.

There was, however, one day in the Deep North when it wasn't frustrating. Grand final day was a special day not only because it was the grand final but because it was broadcast live into Oakey. It was a rare pleasure to just turn the telly on and watch the football without any disruption.

The grand final was exciting and it made me feel funny. I liked how during the national anthem the crowd would cheer earlier and earlier each year so that the band hardly got to the dah-dah-dah-dah in the middle before there was a great roar which had little to do with her majesty, a lot to do with being part of a national event, and a lot more to do with football.

I was lucky not to miss the 1979 grand final. During my last year of high school I worked at the Cecil Café cooking hamburgers and fish and chips. I had a great boss. He thought the $2.22 an hour he paid me was pretty scabby so each night as I was emptying the oil from the friers he'd cook me a mixed grill or a T-bone and salad and we'd have a couple of beers and chat. Sunday nights were especially busy during winter. Blokes would have a few beers at the Oakey footy and then a few more at the Western Line, by which time they knew they were in strife and that there was no chance of tea when they got home. Around closing, which was about 7.30, they'd wander over. 'Give's a hamburger with the lot and a serve of chips thanks.' Then they would stand back from the cabinet of dim sims and Chiko rolls and fish cakes and say, 'Ah, yeah. You might as well throw a bit of that kabana in for us as well.' I'd cut a piece off, put a few nicks in it and toss it into the fat.

I was rostered on to work in the shop on grand final day 1979. When I said I couldn't there was something of an industrial confrontation. Arbitration proved successful and my boss borrowed his mate's portable TV and put it on the soft-drink fridge so I was able to see Wayne Harmes knock that ball back in to Kenny Sheldon to keep Collingwood suffering. I almost liked Carlton that day.

Geelong, of course, was never in a grand final, but I still found it an emotional occasion, though in a different way from every other footy game. Sometimes in the dying minutes of the last quarter, when the result was decided, I found myself with tears in my eyes. There were different kinds of tears; tears of joy for Arnold Breidis and Snake Baker and Frank Gumbleton and for the North Melbourne faithful and tears of grief for the defeated players who sat there after the game with the life sucked out of them. But they were also tears of a pervasive melancholy, a sadness that footy was finished for the year and that we would all go our own ways until we returned in the new year, fresh and clean and hopeful again.

PART 2

a handful of sweetly fluked dancesteps
Peter Goldsworthy, 'Trick Knee'

CHAPTER 8

Oakey had been a good little town to grow up in, but by the time I finished high school I was ready to leave. I wanted to go to uni, and I wanted to go to uni in a place where you didn't need a massive antenna to pick up Channel 7, and where the VFL 'Match of the Day' came through loud and clear and unimpeded. Brisbane was the logical choice.

Life at the University of Queensland started brilliantly. No question, I was in the right place. I had never experienced anything quite like O-Week. Every night there was a party at Union College and each day I ventured onto campus to see what was going on. This was the expansive world I had hoped existed and I was keen to be part of it. Enthusiasts spruiked on behalf of their groups and organisations. You could join the chocolate lovers, the Hare Krishnas, the medieval society, the frisbee chuckers, the lesbian chocolate lovers, the tree-huggers, the life drawing club, the astronomers. There was a Lutheran Students' Fellowship. Even a university branch of the CWA (which I later learnt was the famous Chook-Walkers' Association). If you had a passion you could find someone to share it with. I loved it. I was among vibrant people.

That week I wandered down to the Indoor Sports Pavilion where the Sports and Physical Recreation Association had set up a sporting market place. There were rows of desks and behind each one sat a collection of the clubs' members: one barefoot with his clothes falling off him (the battling student), one in the Queensland Schoolboys' shirt, Adidas tracksuit pants and sunglasses (the wanker), and another in coat and tie (the recent graduate).

I spoke to the cricket club representative who wanted to know at which school I'd played my cricket. When I said Oakey High, he pencilled me in for the fifths. I spoke to the golf club, joined on the spot and organised a game for that Friday afternoon.

I also spoke to the University of Queensland Australian Football Club—the Lions. They had two teams and were part of the strong SQAFA league which included a couple of clubs—Sherwood and Mt Gravatt—that were trying to break into the top level QAFL competition. They wanted to know what footy I had played. Explaining that you were last selected eighth emergency in the Shepparton Under-13s in 1971 when you were nine years old was never going to generate huge approval but they took my name and phone number anyway. When I told them I lived at Union College they laughed and asked, 'Have you met Graeme Mounsey? He plays for us.'

As it turned out I had met him but at Union College he was known as Eric, after Eric Idle. He was also called Mounse. He was in the nth year of a computer science degree (where n is greater than or equal to the designated number of years suggested by the university to complete the course plus one). He had been elected as one of the college social convenors. His willingness to take on the role said as much about his sense of celebrity as it did about his sense of responsibility. He was, however, perfect for the position because he understood the concept of value. When Mounse woke up in the morning he could smell the waft of free departmental wine and cheese and he was known to anatomists, economists, agronomists and philosophers. He had no preference when it came to the various engineering departments. Strangely, few recognised him in the Prentice Centre—the home of Computer Science—which was odd, because Mounse is eminently recognisable. He is about six foot five. Not a Brad Ottens six foot five; more a tall version of Mr Squiggle with Mr XXXX himself in charge of his strings.

Mounse and I quickly discovered we both loved

footy. He had moved around quite a bit during his childhood—Darwin, Kyneton, Rockhampton—and had known the same footy exile I had. He loved Collingwood the same way I loved Geelong. I could tell. During the first few weeks of semester we'd sit and discuss the forthcoming VFL season. Then we'd get onto the season for uni. It'd be great: he'd ruck and I'd work my way round to being first rover. It was possible. Sometimes I'd lie in bed thinking of Kelly Watson but usually I was thinking about football, imagining possession after possession from Mounse's deft taps.

As the season was about to start I faced a huge dilemma. On the one hand I really wanted to play footy. On the other, I had put up with years of that Ming dynasty radiogram and late night TV highlight packages. The prospect of watching live footy every Saturday afternoon was very tempting. What to do? I was coming down on the side of watching. I could always play footy the following year.

Mounse was playing. He was determined and disciplined—but only in those areas of his very rounded life that didn't involve Fortran or Pascal. He went for runs early in the morning and was always keen to get to footy training.

I still couldn't make up my mind. Over a few beers we'd start commentating, 'Mounsey gets the knock to Harms, Harms dummies, he takes a bounce, back to Mounsey. Jeez, Mounse's had a fuckin' air swing.' I started going with him down to the beautiful Number 4

Oval—the home of the mighty University Lions. At one end was the swimming pool and the Brisbane River, on the eastern side the university rainforest, on the western side the gym. At the top end was the Student Rec Club which was built into a hill. In those days it was a grand place for a session, especially on the balcony when footy or cricket was on.

We trained in the same way we studied, doing just enough to get by before heading up for a couple of beers. There was lots of fitness work, lots of skills drills and plenty of circle work. The drills always seemed unnecessarily complicated, as if every evening we had to produce a maypole. We would listen and nod and grunt, substituting collective goodwill for comprehension, then divide ourselves so that there was an equal number of players at each witch's hat. But as footballs flew everywhere and nineteen blokes wound up at one orange cone we would get the standard, 'How the fuck did youse fruitloops get into university?' In keeping with the true spirit of varsity clubs there was very little competitive and physical work, although the only shirt-front I've ever handed out in my life was during a handball drill.

Despite the fact that—not counting house matches in grade four and five—I'd played almost no footy, my skills were passable. Kick-to-kick on the nature strip at Oakey had equipped me to conceal myself among the variety of kicking styles at practice. I could take a mark and could kick the drop punt like they did on TV, but I had no left foot. During the circle work there were penalties for kicking with the wrong foot. I was forever doing push-ups.

Circle work was real footy training. It had all the right noises, 'Nugget, Nugget, Nugget, Nugget, Nugget' and 'Dark, Dark, Dark, Dark' and 'Comin' past' and 'Givit, givit, givit'. Then there was 'Mounse, Mounse, Mounse, Mounse, Mounse' usually followed by 'Fuck. Sorry,' as Mounse sent another short pass west.

For Mounse there was a catalogue of impediments to success where kicking was concerned. He was the sort of player who, even when he had possession of the footy, was rarely in full control of it. That made dropping it the significant distance to his foot difficult. He also lumbered. He had that lower-grade ruckman lumber which gets them to the boundary throw-in at the last instant. He made Mick Nolan look like Ravelomanantsoa. There was also the issue of co-ordination. Mounse could get his hand on a ball-up but when it came to kicking on the run he was in trouble. You could see his eyes spinning around as he wondered how to get foot to ball in between the long, slow strides. He needed a Craig Bradley—someone like me, maybe— to run by *on all occasions* to take the short handball.

But Mounse was one of those players vital to a lower-grade footy team. He had height and a skinny, wiry, Mounsey sort of strength. Ruckmen at this level sacrifice their lanky bodies every Saturday jumping *over* the opposing ruckman (in which case they spend the afternoon being jumped into) or jumping *into* the opposing ruckman. Mounse put in all day. Like a real Collingwood man he never shirked it. He just ran and ran—sometimes in both grades. In fact Mounse was the sort of bloke who'd turn up for a bye.

I still hadn't made a decision about the season, but when Geelong lost the first two games of the season—at home to South by three points and then at Princes Park to Carlton by five—I could feel the frustration mounting. I decided to play for the University Lions.

I missed the first game of the season against Mt Gravatt (we got thrashed) but was picked in the seconds the next week. There were a few nerves on Saturday morning as Mounse and I walked over to Number 4. We got changed—maroon jumper with a white V, maroon shorts and maroon socks. The new boys were welcomed and applauded as everyone marked time, bouncing from foot to foot. The coach tried to rev us up. We weren't really primed for a big performance against South Brisbane. We ran out.

The siren sounded and I remember thinking, 'At last I'm playing football.' It was as if the result didn't matter. It was as if the team didn't matter. It was an altogether self-satisfied feeling. I counted my own kicks, the first of which was a grubber off the left foot which Beckwithed over the boundary line on the half back flank. I just wanted to get the footy and do something with it. Who knows where my opponent was? 'Pick 'em up, Uni. Pick 'em up.' I didn't realise that imperative was directed at me. It didn't mean much in my dreamy reality that here I was actually playing footy for a team, and that that team was trying to win. Who knows what the coach was saying at quarter time? Who knows what the game plan was? I didn't even know the names of some of my team-mates.

I was given a run on the ball and this little bloke who was about forty just kept getting possessions—and doing something with them. He tore us to shreds. Well, he tore me to shreds and I had a stint on the bench and the game was over, and we'd been flogged. But it was a game of footy. The heads hung low in the dressing room as we got the mandatory roasting, 'You blokes were pissweak out there today. It's the start of the season and fair dinkum, you blokes might as well not bother turnin' up if that's how yuh gunna play all fuckin' year. Are yuh gunna put in or are yuh just gunna run round?' I felt like putting up my hand and saying I was more than happy to just run around; that I had been waiting for this all my life; that the highlight for me was seeing my name on a team sheet, and that eight kicks and one handball in my first game wasn't too bad. But it was inappropriate to interrupt. 'Are we gunna fuckin' put in like Mounse?' the coach continued. 'Look at him. He's given everything. Look at him. How do you feel when you look over at Mounse?'

I felt like saying I felt like a couple of beers but this wouldn't have been appropriate either. Mounse looked like a country handicapper who's finished fourth in the

Melbourne Cup and is walking back along the path through the roses at Flemington. He had his guernsey off, elbows on knees, head in hands, still dripping sweat, bruised, scratched, blistered and when he got up he was all proppy.

We clearly weren't a uni club in the tradition of Melbourne or Adelaide where the lower-grade teams include economics professors and sculptors and political activists who love footy and take it in turns to make witty three-quarter-time addresses relating footy to Benthamite Utilitarianism, Pindar and the Beatitudes.

I suspect I was in love with the *idea* of playing footy as much as I was in love with playing footy. In reality footy was actually rough and tumble, and pain and hard work, and other things less than necessary.

For the next couple of games my name appeared on the team sheet. I liked going over to the ISP on the way to the rec club to see the oval diagram with the names in position. I liked all the footy things associated with being in a footy team. Out on the ground, however, I had little idea where the ball was. It seemed to be sailing back over my head just as I was getting to where I thought I should be. Mounse didn't have enough breath to offer advice but the runner did. 'Come and have a spell.' I got a few kicks, flew for a few marks, chased my opponent. We'd lose.

If we played at home I didn't hang around for the

firsts. Geelong was working its way into the season. They were having one of those years where they start to play some brilliant footy and you can't help yourself, you start to feel that real sense of hope. Not the hope things will go well, but that sense which pushes you into dangerous territory—you feel yourself believing in the Geelong Football Club. The choice was getting harder: play for the University Lions or watch the Cats on TV.

I stuck with the Lions. Mounse was encouraging. ('You weak shit: what d'you want to give footy away for?') We showed signs of improvement against Acacia Ridge, keeping with them for the first half. Mounse didn't have such a great day after his opponent grabbed the crotch of his shorts and ripped it out, telling him to fuck off and then holding the piece of material aloft like Caligula. This sort of incident not only helped me come to an understanding of the nature of humanity, it also helped me find another yard of pace. I got the ball a bit more and started to work out how to make a little time once I had it. Mounse even commented, 'You're getting the hang of it.' We couldn't win a game though. Geelong could. They kept North scoreless after quarter time one day. They were flogging everyone.

I was picked on the wing for the away match against Strathpine, a suburb on the northern outskirts of Brisbane. It was wet—most unusual for Brisbane winter. It had rained all night and was still dark and overcast as we drove out in Mounse's Ford Escort. The ground was your classic Moorabbin gluepot right down the middle of the ground and it had sheets of water on the wings. It was still spitting. And it was cold.

For some reason the away team's shed wasn't available so we had to share with Strathpine. A makeshift divider kept the two teams apart. As the ankles were strapped and the liniment went on, we showed impeccable manners. Our proximity had no effect on the Strathpine boys. They had plenty to say. These were the days when uni students were long-haired commie bastards, and all opposing teams were of the view that we were soft. *Ipso facto* most sides wanted to bash the billy goats out of us. They hated us. 'They're soft, these uni faggots,' a voice thundered from beyond the divide. 'Let's get out there and hammer the bastards.'

We run on, through the puddles and into the mud. I sort of tippy-toe and sidestep the sloppy stuff, trying not to get dirty. We warm up and it is still drizzling. I take up my position on the wing. My opponent comes over to me. He is short and fat and he has no neck. I put out my hand and say, 'Have a good game, mate.' He spits at it, looks at me and says, 'Don't come near me all fuckin' day you smartarse little shit.' I am happy with this arrangement.

I am taller than him but lighter and about half his age. He is angry because he thinks I am going to be a doctor or a barrister. I feel it might be in my best interests to point out that I'm actually a failing maths student and I'd be more than happy to work alongside him at the Golden Circle cannery. He is one of those well-tummied men whose shorts button points more downwards than outwards and he has the pointy, balletic feet which some fat men and Wayne Harmes have.

The game starts and after about two and half minutes and six ball-ups Mounse is covered in mud. He's copped one in the knees, one in the noggin and one in the nuts and he's thinking there's only another two hours of this to go. The coach is having a shot at him when Mounse gets onto one and thumps the ball out to my wing. I am standing well clear of my opponent who I have realised looks like Henry VIII's fat cousin. We both run at the ball, only he is running at the ball *and* at me. Before I know it my body moves without me telling it to. I prop, and my arm stretches out for the Sherrin. Henry's cousin has committed himself to all-out violence. As he arrives I find myself in the classic Dick Reynolds-*Football-the-Australian-Way*-Scanlen's-footy-cards-photograph position—ball about to be dragged in. I snap it away from him and he pummels the space where me and the ball were going to be. He falls over, hits the puddle and aquaplanes on the apex of his tummy. Water flies everywhere. As I pull the ball in, I spin 360 degrees onto my left foot and send a pop pass thirty metres to the full forward who has led straight out from goal. It hits his chest and he goes back and kicks a goal. I know that I have made precisely the right movements. I also know that I have had no control over what has happened. I will play so little footy that these few fluked dancesteps, as poet

Peter Goldsworthy once called them, will stay in my memory forever. They will be evidence for my argument that there is a footy instinct for the simple reason that I have never learnt to do what I have just done. I also know how good it has made me feel—and has made others feel. A few players come over and hit me on the bum.

The rain stops and during the course of the afternoon the Strathpine seconds (average age thirty-two) get madder and madder. We stay with them. The scoreboard says we are two points down in time-on in the last quarter: 6.10 to 6.8. The crowd watches. You can hear the Strathpine followers screaming; you can hear them groaning as their forward thrusts are thwarted.

We clear the ball out of the back line. I lead off the wing. The footy bounces into my arms. I don't have to break stride. I streak away from my opponent who has got his head down as his arms pump and he turns on a wider arc than mine. I thump the ball forward and it is marked by our centre half forward who has led across the ground. He's well clear. I yell for him to run on. But he has no left foot, so he pulls up. I keep running. My opponent has stopped chasing. I run past for the handball. Our centre half forward doesn't give it. He is forty-five metres out. He goes back and takes forever to kick for goal. He thinks he can be a hero but the footy is saturated. It is so heavy that it has become a lethal weapon which violates about four articles of the Geneva Convention. He won't make it past the top of the square. The siren is about to go. The forward line fills with bodies. Even I keep running forward. He's goin' the torp. He launches. It's one of those mongrel punts which, from the instant it leaves the boot, is only ever going to land in one person's arms. I am standing in a crowded forward line but there is never any doubt—this one has my name all over it. It dips and drops and I take it on the chest. With seconds to go I am fifteen metres out in the pocket on a forty-five-degree angle. Team-mates come from everywhere. They offer advice. Opponents mill around like salivating wolves. I feel like giggling. I haven't played in a winning team all season. I'm on the right side for a right footer. I aim to the right of centre of the goals. It stays there. It goes straight over the top of the goalpost. The goal umpire signals a minor score. We are still a point behind. I have had my chance. I feel bad. The boys are disappointed. From the kick-out we scramble another point. The siren goes. It's a draw. We are jubilant. The Strathpine players look like they're going to kill us.

It gets worse. The goal umpires confer in the middle and start looking officious. They cross their flags at the scoreboard. We find out that we have actually won by a point 6.11 to 6.10. We head into the changerooms arm in arm and gather in a circle to sing the club song:

Drunk last night, drunk the night before,
Gunna get drunk tonight like we've never been drunk
before,
Cos here we are, happy as can be,

We are the boys of the var-sitt-tee.
Glorious, victorious, one jug of beer between the four of
    us,
Thank God there are no more of us,
Cos one of us could drink the bloody lot (without his
    pants on)
One of us could drink the bloody lot (roll over Mabel)
Your navel's on the other side.
You beauty, you beauty, you beauty

None of us has considered the sensitivity of the geopolitical situation. As we are congratulating each other and working out where the first beer is going to come from there is an almighty crash on the divider—a bit like the axe in *The Shining*. Mounse and I decide a shower is superfluous to life's basic needs at this time so we drive back to Brisbane covered in Strathpine mud— and glory. Geelong also win.

That night Mounse found a party to crash. He was a genius at finding parties. We were in such high spirits that we bought a forty of Bundy and headed off. We knocked on the door of an old Queenslander in Toowong. For once Mounse had dud info. It was a dinner party of eight. We didn't know anyone. We apologised for interrupting and were shown the door. As the guests left about three hours later we were sitting quietly on the front steps drinking rumbos and reliving the match.

I still had mud on my legs.

CHAPTER 9

Geelong were going well that year. They had a great run through June and July. In fact they were doing so well that after the Mt Gravatt thugs tried to kill us, I wondered whether it was worth continuing as a lower-grades university footballer. They beat us by 156 points in a game where our entire score of 0.6.6 was kicked by Evan Ackermann. I wound up at centre half back—all 66 kg and 180 cm of me (I had grown about twenty centimetres in grade twelve)—and an expat Victorian laughed when I came out to pick him up after three-quarter time. He told me he was from down south and was actually being paid to play. Before the ball-up he stood on my foot to trap me. He was successful. He was heavy. He wanted to see what I would do about it. I tried to push him off but he just laughed, kept standing on my foot and pushed me back. I felt like one of those weighted, plastic inflatable toys that you get at service stations that can't be pushed over. Why did blokes want to kill you in second grade SQAFA footy?

Geelong won ten in a row which convinced me that watching the VFL on TV was far more attractive than being one of those toys. So I decided to bow out of club footy for a while. Mounse kept at it while I stayed home to watch Channel 7's 'Match of the Day'.

A few of us at Union College would sit and watch on Saturday afternoons. The dominant character in the TV room was a struggling law student called Gulbo. He was also a struggling Collingwood supporter and a great mate of Mounse's. Four years my senior, he exercised freely his right to put shit on me for being a Geelong supporter, a Lutheran and a first year. He was very good at it, which is probably why he is now a successful barrister. In those days Gulbo was a Collingwood yobbo who knew a few lines of Shakespeare. For the son of sound Irish Catholic working-class stock from Sarina in northern Queensland, Gulbo gave a great impression of someone who had lived in Melbourne. He was a first-class abuser of umpires, and a top-shelf berater of his own players when they failed under pressure. Towards the end of the home and away season Collingwood was under a lot of pressure while the Cats were still looking strong. This did not sit nicely with Gulbo's view of the world. Our teams met in round twenty with the Pies desperately needing a win to make the five. I had all but forgotten the University Football Club existed. Geelong quickly got on top and looked like staying there. Gulbo had lots of old sayings and he loved using them. It was as if he always wanted to be the bloke in the porkpie hat sitting at the bar striking a match, lighting a fag and looking at you. He called girls 'sheilas' and he'd say things like, 'She's a good lookin' sheila, that one. Mate, she'd put a horn on a house cow.' Gulbo was also a great one for hurling his thong at the TV when a decision went against Collingwood— a rare event—or when one of his players erred. That afternoon the thong was projected at the telly numerous times and once he actually turned the set off. 'They're bloody hopeless.' Geelong won and I was held responsible.

Somehow Collingwood scrambled into the five. The Cats finished on top. This was looking like *the* year, and if it was *the* year I had to be at the MCG to be part of it. We were one win away from the grand final. Gulbo, Mounse and I decided we'd go to Melbourne for the big day. We made the necessary arrangements. Collingwood, miraculously, kept winning. But Geelong lost to Richmond in the major semi. This meant that Geelong and Collingwood were to meet in the preliminary final.

Gulbo was seeing this as a great personal battle.

We gathered in the darkness of the Union College

TV room. There were no beers. It was too serious for beer. It was an even first half. Gulbo was surprisingly quiet. The Cats got on top in the third quarter but it didn't show on the scoreboard. Gulbo was getting the thong mobile. Scores were pretty well level but it looked like we were going to go into three-quarter time ahead and then run away with the game. I felt quietly confident.

Quiet confidence is a wholly inappropriate feeling when you are a Geelong supporter. Just as I was feeling good about life the Cats went to sleep in time-on. Ronnie Wearmouth kicked a couple of quick goals and not only did Collingwood hit the front, the Cats looked like they had the staggers. Their belief was shot. And mine was under serious threat. The last quarter was awful. You could feel the Geelong nerves. You could see them fighting their doubt. Gary Malarkey tried to steady them. They came back. They got within a goal but Collingwood hung on. Pies by four.

It was too much. I felt as crook as a Geelong supporter. And didn't Gulbo let me know what a bunch of handbaggers the Cats really were. He acted in the finest tradition of the Collingwood winner.

Footy was over for the season for me. I just couldn't bring myself to go to the grand final. Geelong: we were a bunch of losers.

Mounse and Gulbo were winners. They caught the second-class sitter to Sydney and then on to Melbourne, clickety-clacking all the way with the expectation of a Magpie premiership. To anaesthetise themselves for the journey Mounse had procured a beaker of ethanol from the chemistry department. I have a picture in my mind of two mad Collingwood supporters somewhere around Uranquinty mixing pure alcohol and green cordial to make a concoction they called Green Death, excited, three-parts tanked and playing their role in the winning of a Magpie flag.

I watched the game on TV thinking of the pilgrims. I loved them like brothers. But, jeez, I hated Collingwood. I cheered Kevin Bartlett. Geoff Raines was all class. I even found myself sympathetic to the performance of David Cloke. I delighted that Collingwood were thrashed by a record margin: eighty-one points.

The next day, as the boys pushed out of Melbourne nursing hangovers I was racing around uni writing '81' in as many places as I could. I chalked it up in some great spots. You'd walk around a corner, and there on the physio ramp would be a number two metres tall: 81. It must have taken me hours. Some of those letters remained until the next year.

During the 1981 season it always seemed to be Carlton on TV; great games where Wayne Johnston stirred the souls of those in the Heatley Stand, Peter Bosustow leapt all over packs, Ken Hunter was braver than you could imagine anyone being and Bruce Doull was just Bruce Doull.

Geelong didn't have a team of champions but we had a lot of blokes with red hair like Scratcher Neal and Neville Bruns and John Mossop. Gulbo described Geelong as a team which had been hit with the ugly stick. But we beat Essendon in the last round at VFL Park to pinch third place from them and Fitzroy flogged the Maggies to deny them top spot. Gulbo's thong was flying around the room as Fitzroy led 5.9 to 0.2 at half time. I loved it. We would play Collingwood in the qualifying final.

My rivalry with Gulbo was poorly imitated in the real sports world. Borg and McEnroe, Nicklaus and Watson, Celtic and Rangers—they had nothing on us. Gulbo hadn't forgiven me for a youthful indiscretion earlier that year. We were at the Queensland–New South Wales State of Origin match at Lang Park. State of Origin was in its second year. We stood with a one-eyed Queensland crowd on the terraces drinking the local product. The ground was packed. Not long into the game New South Wales led 15–0. The Maroons looked gone but fought back and won the game 24–15. It was one of the great sporting contests. We danced. In our euphoria we decided to jump the fence and run across Lang Park. These were the days when you still could.

Gulbo negotiated the fence and, can in hand, rolled along, his large frame gathering momentum. Filled with Origin bravado I tackled him right around the ankles. It was one of those tackles where you don't even see the player go from upright to arse up. Gulbo hit the deck. The first point of contact with the ground was the can in his hand. Beer geysered up. It was pretty funny. Gulbo got up and brushed the grass off. 'Stupid little prick' was what he said I think. And then nothing. In the car going home it was strangely quiet. Too quiet. I'd had a few too many to realise something was up. When we arrived back at college Gulbo got me in a headlock and the lads relieved me of all of my garments. They then set me free, naked, in the grounds of the university.

What was I to do? How would I explain this to security if they spotted me, or, worse still, to the nuns at Duchesne College? I decided to buy time and sprinted to the Number 1 Oval where I hid behind the sightscreen. Word got out that I was somewhere in the university grounds and I remember a search party of about thirty coming my way. They reminded me of a lynch mob. I made a break, sidestepped a few of them and then found myself face to face with one of the college wardens. He handed me a towel.

A few of us had created a Saturday afternoon ritual: a lazy lunch in the college dining room—something like battered savs with salad—and then we'd sit on the rocks outside the dining room with a cup of tea. Then down to the TV room. The Queensland telecast started in the studio with anchors Ken Hose and Bruce Burgoyne. Gulbo was, as always, impatient: 'Just cross you deadshits,' he'd yell.

The line would come up and Ken Hose would say, 'I think we can go down there now Bruce.' Suddenly we would be plonked into Windy Hill or Waverley and the teams would be warming up and Lou would be trying not to sound like a Collingwood supporter.

Geelong won that qualifying final, but lost to Carlton in the second semi-final. We played the Pies again in the preliminary. Surely this time. Imagine the Cats beating Carlton to win the flag. On Saturday morning I loved them. By late that afternoon Gulbo was giving me heaps—again. We lost—again. It was the famous match where Gary Sidebottom failed to meet the bus and Peter Johnston was called in as a replacement at the last minute. On the way to the game he'd stopped for lunch at a hamburger joint. Theories abound as to what he ordered—everything from two dim sims and a serve of chips to a steakburger with the works, a Polly Waffle and a pine-lime Splice. There is no argument over the sitter he missed from the goal square, right at a crucial time. Again all day Geelong looked like they were about to get away, but Collingwood fought back in the last quarter and won.

Mounse and Gulbo decided they needed to get to the grand final again. They managed to talk their mate JT into driving them. He had graduated and was the proud owner of a new Celica. Not far out of Brisbane they hit a magpie which sadly disintegrated. As they looked back at the cloud of feathers they knew that the trip was to be futile.

Carlton fought back in the last quarter to win the flag.

At the start of each season I talked about playing for the University Lions again although I never did. I found 'Match of the Day' more attractive than playing. I was also playing a lot of golf. In the final years of my extended history degree I would play golf on Saturday morning and watch Geelong get flogged in the afternoon. We struggled for the next couple of seasons but we could also be brilliant at times. This was so Geelong.

There were a couple of big footy games at the Gabba in the early eighties. Richmond played Carlton in an exhibition match for the Commonwealth Games and there was a home and away match between Essendon and Hawthorn which drew a huge crowd. We sat on the greyhound track in the sunshine and abused Don Scott and Leigh Matthews. These days there's no dog track at the Gabba and Leigh Matthews is a hero in Brisbane.

Spud Murphy and I would wander over to Wests' home ground at Chelmer late some Sunday afternoons when it was free to get in. Spud was in the fifth year of his philosophy degree—just beyond half-way. He had grown up on rugby union but his scholarly toil had revealed the truth and he had started to take an interest in the VFL. He followed North Melbourne.

Wests were coached by an old Collingwood player, one of the side that had beaten Geelong in the 1980 preliminary final. I blamed that team for everything that was wrong with Geelong in those days. They had started the rot. If they hadn't taken the heart out of us we might well have won that flag and the culture of the club and the nature of its spectators would have been different. Those Collingwood players made me a different person; they prevented us from winning those grand finals in the nineties.

I remember the first time we went to Chelmer to watch Wests in 1984. Spud lives close to the ground and we feel like a Sunday arvo beer so we stroll over. I get the beers and we go and stand on the bank with the sun behind us. We're chatting away half watching the footy and I see this creature with long frizzy blond hair running around in a Wests jumper. I spray beer everywhere. I point and I get all agitated: I am as close to a Collingwood player as I've been since I first went to the VFL footy with the Hogans. I explain it all to Spud.

We get another beer and wander out to the huddle for a closer look. He looks like something out of AC/DC. He looks like he should be wearing tight Levis out on the field. He is so skinny it is difficult to believe he could have been part of any top side, let alone the one that maimed Geelong in 1980.

He begins his three-quarter-time address. He calls the boys in. 'Youse blokes. Fuckin' get in 'ere. Get in fuckin' close.' He pauses. A long pause. He looks at the clipboard and then gives it to the trainer. He starts with his head down. 'That was fuckin' shithouse. And youse all fuckin' know it. Fuck me, youse pricks want a fuckin' bomb up y'arse.' He lifts his head. 'Do youse know anything 'bout fuckin' football? Anything? Because Christ Almighty yuh don't look like yuh do. Youse are fuckin' massacrin' the game I love. I fuckin' love this game. That's why I'm here, why I'm fuckin' here. I love football. And I wanna love this fuckin' football club.'

Most of his comments are supported with projections of spittle and the circle slowly moves backwards.

'The thing is youse know what the fuckin' problem is. Youse all fuckin' know it. The fuckin' problem is youse don't love footy enough. I fuckin' know that for a fuckin' fact. Cos if youse loved footy youse woodna played like the pack of fuckin' sheilas yuh were for most of that quarter. Jesus fuckin' Christ.'

Spud has never seen anything like this. Is this the glorious game, the glorious culture I've been describing to him over cask red in the wee small hours of the night?

'Blue, what the fuck are you doin' kickin' across the face a goal? What's wrong with Robbo? He's been free all fuckin' day. What's he got fuckin' crabs or something? Spot 'im and fuckin' hit 'im. We've gotta think fellas. We've got brains; we've just gotta fuckin' use 'em.'

The circle moves further back.

'This is what we're gunna do. Youse pricks are gunna restore a bitta fuckin' pride. Youse are gunna get to the fuckin' pill first and if that doesn't happen yuh gunna put some physical fuckin' pressure on your man. For Chrissake don't just fuckin' present it to 'im. Make 'im fuckin' earn it.'

He thinks. He softens and then he closes. 'Come on fellas. They're not much chop this mob. Fuck, Macca got half a dozen touches that quarter. If Macca can get his hands on the fuckin' leather any prick can.'

Macca sees this as a compliment. Spud doesn't.

'Let's just get out there and play football. Let's at least fuckin' show that we've got a bit of passion for the game. Let's go Wests.'

There is the standard roar of support.

It is such a performance that Spud and I go to quite a few home games. We arrive just before three-quarter time and listen to Bon Scott abusing the players. Sometimes we don't even stay to the end of the final quarter. Wests start to play some pretty good footy but Bon is always as prickly and the circle never gets any tighter.

I would stand there thinking about how things change; how far away Chelmer was from Princes Park in Shepparton; how life can take you all over the place but somehow you keep coming back to footy.

CHAPTER 10

By the time I'd finished my arts degree I didn't know very much at all. The few history lectures I attended showed me human folly and human tragedy. So did the Geelong Football Club. The books I read and the films I saw directed me to contemplate the struggle between good and evil. So did Saturday afternoon matches between Geelong and Collingwood. I could listen to Paul Simon's 'American Tune' and feel the sadness. I could listen to the commentary of a match from Kardinia Park and feel the same thing.

Football, I was starting to realise, was about many things; more things than I had ever consciously thought as a child. When you are a child footy has an effect on you. It makes you feel things, think things, know things. Only you don't realise that footy is having an effect on you. You just experience it all.

When you have spent over twenty years suffering the Geelong Football Club you begin to think about it. Why are you able to start each season with renewed hope? Where does that come from? You start to believe there is more to the game. I loved footy, deeply. It was part of me; in me. But why?

These moments of contemplation were fleeting, however. There were more important things to consider. Like, what was I going to do now that I'd finished my arts degree? I still lived in Brisbane. I was readying myself for a summer of club cricket and wondering about the future. I thought I would teach for a while and then, when the time was right and I was a bit more motivated, I'd go back to uni and study something properly. It was all very vague.

There was one thing I was sure of. I was going to play footy. I was going to have at least one full season—somewhere. I couldn't go through life without ever giving it a go.

While I was at uni in Brisbane my parents and David and Mick moved to Eudunda, a little village of German Lutherans about half an hour out of the Barossa Valley in South Australia. I loved visiting the old stone home with its fireplaces and verandahs and grapevines and beautiful garden.

I was offered a place in the 1985 Dip. Ed. course at Flinders University. This was a great opportunity to study education (or at least do enough to get the bit of paper at the end) and to go to Adelaide to catch up with the family. It was also a chance to play footy.

David was at Adelaide Uni studying medicine. He had picked up footy pretty quickly at Immanuel College. All those afternoons playing kick-to-kick at Oakey had given him a reasonable base and, despite an average kicking style, he made the firsts. At uni he and a few mates had signed up with the Adelaide Lutheran Football Club, which was then being hammered by most of the sides in the southern churches' leagues. I was very keen to join him and we would have a season together experiencing the joys of footy. At last.

This meant leaving Brisbane. I packed everything I owned into two Wridgways cartons, threw my cricket bag and golf clubs in my Mini Moke and headed south. It was an epic two-day journey, top down, the Stones and Dean Martin cranking out from the cassette player on the seat next to me. I survived a rather close lightning strike outside Dubbo, a plague of locusts on the Hay Plain which clogged the radiator and caused the engine to overheat, and a crumbed sausage at Merbein South. I was in footy country again. I passed the footy oval in Euston and that classic oval at Lake Cullulleraine. I imagined the contests played on them; contests which warranted one line in the Melbourne papers.

I crossed the border into South Australia. It's amazing how a few different coloured number plates and a fruit-fly bin can make you feel like you're in a new state. South

Australians had their own way; their own language. They were fiercely proud of their footy in Adelaide and of the fact that they had provided many champions in the VFL. They resented the Victorian belief that Melbourne was the centre of the footy universe.

The welcome sign at the bottom of the Eudunda hill said, 'YOU ARE ENTERING ROOSTER TERRI-TORY' an inspired greeting designed to make you feel at home if you were a local or make you fearfully aware of the prowess and influence of the Eudunda FC if you weren't.

Over the summer David and I worked in the Eudunda silos. We emptied the grain trucks and talked about Kim Hughes and beer and golf and how good the footy season was going to be. On the weekends we played cricket for the local club. We made the semis, but were beaten by Tanunda at their home ground. As the older team members sat around in the grandstand wondering how we'd managed to lose we'd moved on. We had the footy out. Kick-to-kick. It was only a few weeks to go.

In country towns footy and cricket are part of life. My brother played cricket for Chiltern for a while. While batting one day he was standing at the striker's end. The return from the boundary went to the bowler's end. As the huge throw headed in the bowler saw that he was in the perfect position to take a speccie. He jumped, put his knee on the shoulder of the non-striker, climbed into the air and pulled down a classic high mark. Boys will *never* forgo a speccie opportunity.

David and I stayed at Luther Seminary in North Adelaide. The sem, as everyone called it, was one of those ivy-clad colonial buildings which make you feel like you should wear jackets with elbow patches, ride bicycles, go to evensong and read C. S. Lewis. It was where blokes spent seven years studying to be pastors. There were not enough sem students, however, to fill the residences so the principal, Dr Harman, took in tertiary students. Some sem students didn't appreciate card-playing, beer-drinking, lecture-avoiding tertiary students around the place. Others didn't mind. Some budding young theologians were very much aware of the spiritual benefits of a full house, a full fridge and a full night's rest. Generally people got on pretty well.

Footy was a great tradition of Luther Seminary. There was often a game of kick-to-kick in Wellington Square before dinner and I can assure you that sem students presented with a speccie opportunity didn't always demonstrate Christian charity. They had no problem putting the knee wherever it was necessary in the interest of propelling themselves heavenward.

Sem was the Assumption College of the Adelaide Lutheran Football Club. Many of its residents were stalwarts of the mighty Bulldogs—and I was thrilled to be joining them. That year the ALFC moved into the Adelaide Amateur Football League which had eleven divisions, each with ten teams. In addition, eight of those eleven divisions had reserve grade competitions.

That meant that in 1985 there were in total 190 senior amateur footy teams. Add to that the hundreds of junior clubs and school teams and you see how significant footy was in Adelaide at that time—and still is. Adelaide Lutheran fielded teams in the A6, A6 reserves, and A11 divisions.

At the first training I met the A-grade coach Ian Williams. Like most people with the name 'Williams' in lower grades footy in South Australia he was known only as 'Fos' after the legendary Port Adelaide coach. Our Fos was a teacher; kind-hearted and comparatively gentle by footy standards. He was in his thirties; one of those blokes who still had a beard from his student days. You could imagine him at a Vietnam moratorium or in a chocolate velvet dinner jacket at his wedding. He loved the blokes, and he loved the Adelaide Lutheran Footy Club. David introduced me. Fos turned to David, 'Your brother, heh. Does he kick like you?'

Fos was always looking for something new and the night he introduced circle work in both directions simultaneously was well remembered. It was a failure. Mal Thiele was carried off in an ugly collision and never played again—that was one less player to be considered at the famous port-fuelled selectors' meetings.

The A-grade squad was made up of all types. There were quite a few of those natural sportsmen: blokes who were fit and strong and quick and who moved elegantly and had great skills. They could kick with both feet and hit a cover drive and a backhand and would thrash you at ping-pong and pinball. They looked a million bucks and had been invited down to the Norwood Under-19s which is where they learnt a lot about themselves and the world.

Then there were those who weren't quite as flashy but who looked like they'd had a footy in their hands all their lives. Some of these blokes were from the country. There were the more robust, rugged, run-through-you-and-put-you-in-hospital types of which Adelaide Lutheran had about one. His name was Bobby Brady, a reformed crim who'd been inside. All the A-graders and the more talented B-graders were in that squad—it was a squad of blokes who could play.

I trained with the leftovers who would make up the Bs and Cs.

As a collection of youngish men we showed that God had imagination. There were blokes of all shapes and sizes: short, fat blokes with a strip of hairy tummy showing; skinny blokes who walked with the syncopated gait of a stoned camel; blokes who squinted because they left their glasses in the dressing shed; round blokes who ran as if they were hobbled; blokes who went '*Sssss….Sssss…Sssss*' when they sprinted. We trained under the watchful guidance of Tubo, the oversized Adelaide copper who coached the Bs, and Gary Feger who coached the Cs.

Sometimes the whole club would train together. As Fos talked to us I'd cast my eye around at all the different jumpers. They announced an allegiance:

home-town jumpers, school jumpers, SANFL or VFL club jumpers; long sleeves, short sleeves, short sleeves with a T-shirt underneath. And footy shorts. These were the days when to be a young bloke in South Australia meant you had a couple of pairs of very small, tight, elastic, almost-shiny footy shorts. They were an all-purpose fashion item: good not only for footy but also for wearing to Woolworths, to the pub, to the cricket at Adelaide Oval, swimming down the Bay or water-skiing up the Murray.

As the weeks went by we started to get fit. There was heaps of circle work and even the B-grade squad was starting to show a hint of form. We did a bit of competitive stuff. I found myself up against Munch, one of the first years from sem, who looked about twelve and a half: skinny, pimply and not yet in the market for a disposable razor. Five years his senior, I assumed I would have no trouble with the young fella. But I couldn't get near the ball. His body was always in a place which kept me away and he knew exactly when to accelerate and how to twist and step to get away. He knew footy. Munch was soon training with the A-graders. A few years later, as Adelaide Lutheran won a few flags and worked its way up the grades, Munch won the Association best and fairest.

David trained with the A-grade but some of his best mates trained with us. Stolly looked like Fred Flintstone and was studying electrical engineering. Unfortunately he hadn't been blessed with the greatest footy skills. Still he loved footy and he loved Adelaide Lutheran and he'd worked out how to make the most of what he had. He trained and played with his mouth wide open and once against Ferryden Park the pig leather nearly disappeared when he ran at it from full back like David Dench and it hit him in the face. He was prone to straight-lined, stiff-fingered attacks on the ball, but he was effective in an Adelaide Lutheran A6 reserves sort of way. Stolly had other God-given talents, particularly when it came to having fun.

It seemed we were always talking about footy. Plenty of stories flew around the dinner table at sem and even more at the Wellington Hotel, which was a whole two hundred metres down the road. It was owned by former South Adelaide legend Peter Darley.

Others from sem signed up. Heiko Denke, an engineering student from South Africa had spent a lifetime playing soccer. We called him Zulu. He was tall, athletic and fit, but he kicked the footy like Pat Jennings or Mervyn Day—throwing it up and out in front of him and giving it a thump. He was determined to overcome this cultural impediment and developed a kicking style which drew on the inspiration of Curly Austin.

Boof also decided to sign on. He didn't live at sem but he'd gone to school in the Barossa with a few guys who did. Boof was one of those blokes who, having finished school, dabbled with the armed forces to feed some of his childhood obsessions. He walked around in a trench coat, even when it was hot, and no one would have been surprised to see him on the seven o'clock news being hauled away by the police after a siege at the uni laundromat. He was a cross between the green-keeper in *Caddyshack* and Robert Duvall in *Apocalypse Now* who loved the smell of napalm in the morning. He went on to study law.

Then there was young Bongo who'd learnt his footy and his Lutheran faith in the Riverina—at The Rock. He was a first-year chemistry student; a lean, fit kid from the bush who loved footy and had some go in him.

On Thursday nights after training we'd wind up at the Welly. In those days Grenville Dietrich, the last of the old fashioned full forwards, could be found there on Friday nights preparing for his SANFL match the next day. These were pre-Crows days when South Australian footy still held the committed focus of the state's footy fans. It was clean footy. Open. Lacking pressure, although sometimes it could be spiteful. South Australians made it clear that they did not view Melbourne as the centre of the football universe. But most of them had a VFL club they followed.

A shout at the Welly was usually four beers and J4 (Del Shannon's 'Runaway') on the jukebox and the place would buzz with happy students trying to make themselves appear more attractive than they really were. By eleven the shout would be four rums and J4 on the jukebox and you'd be fumbling in your pocket hoping the five coins and two notes had miraculously replenished themselves.

At the end of the night the gathering would head down to O'Connell Street to one of the hamburger joints for a dose of grease. We preferred the Boss Shop, so named because the Elvis clones who worked there called everyone 'Boss'. They'd greet everyone with: 'How you goin' Boss,' and then turn to another Elvis: 'Hey, Boss is here.' They called me Queensland Boss and always put a pineapple ring on my hamburger with bacon and egg (saved getting up early for breakfast). Clearly we were concerned for our fitness.

The first practice match was at a ground on South Road. I had a run in the seconds and was pleased to get a few touches in the opening minutes of the first quarter—a couple of scrubby kicks and a handball to Justin Heyne which resulted in a goal. This was exactly what was supposed to happen. I got a few more kicks. My opponent got more. It was good fun. Everyone got a bit of a run. We got beaten. Still, it was a start.

The big news that afternoon was that Geelong had beaten Hawthorn, the previous year's grand finalist, in the opening round of the season. Later that night we saw the highlights at the Welly. The pub was bubbling with that unmistakable post-match euphoria. It was the first time I remember really noticing Gary Ablett, seeing what the fuss was about.

It is a sunny day at Waverley. The Geelong colours stir the soul—again. I have been so focused on the Adelaide Lutheran Football Club that I have forgotten how much I love the Cats. They move the ball brilliantly. Ablett is everywhere. At one point there is a large pack of players about fifty metres out from goal. Ablett smashes through them. Some players are skittled, others contest the footy. Ablett doesn't really take possession of the footy—he sort of kicks it out of the air from forty-five metres and it sails through. 'Did you see that?' They replay this incident a lot during the season. The Cats kick twenty and win by five goals. I have played football. I have had a few touches. I'm with the boys having a beer. The Cats look great. Gary Ablett is remarkable. All is well with the world.

The next week Collingwood beats us by twenty-odd points at home. We don't win again until round five.

On Sunday mornings we sat together in the North Adelaide Lutheran church. We hoped for short sermons and we'd wander back to the TV room at sem to watch the various footy panels analyse the matches from the day before.

We would also talk about the Adelaide Lutheran Football Club. It was an unusual footy club. A lot of those who played had had text card books when we were kids, we had all been to Sunday School picnics and junior youth, we could all sing 'A Mighty Fortress

Is Our God', we could all still recite Luther's explanation of the third article of the Apostles' Creed. And we loved 'World of Sport' and the footy replay; we knew that Michael Aish would never make it in the VFL and that Peter Motley would.

A couple of weeks before the first round of the season there would be spontaneous singing of the Adelaide Lutheran club song—outside the dining room, in the second-floor showers, walking down to Adelaide Uni, and especially at the Welly. The girls from Lutheran Teachers' College thought we were just boys. We were having fun. Stolly's inability to hold a note never precluded him from leading the throng.

A Bulldog for me,
A Bulldog for me,
If you're not a Bulldog
You're no good to me;
The others will fall,
Cos they're too bloody old,
But the mighty old Bulldogs
The pride of them all.

In the lead-up to the first match we trained hard on the Thursday night. On the Friday night we thought it best we have a quiet one. Stolly, David and I were picked in the seconds for the opening round. I was a little disappointed: I was on the bench.

We had a couple of beers while we tucked into one of those fantastic square pizzas from O'Connell Street. The game was played over and over. We were gunna do this and gunna do that. We had a few more beers but we were home not long after midnight.

The game was against Campbelltown–Magill, on a huge ground used by the East Torrens Cricket Club. David liked this idea. The bigger the ground, the more opportunity we had to find a bit of space. All we had to do was keep running. We were a young and keen side; we could do that.

We togged up. In those days Adelaide Lutheran wore North Melbourne colours and I was given the Phil Krakouer jumper: number 8. I loved how the Krakouers played footy. As Jack Dyer said, 'He's a good player, the Krakouer brothers.' There was some tape and a bit of Deep Heat flying around but it was pretty low-key in the dressing room. There were plenty of short, sharp handballs, and a few firm little kicks. Stolly looked amused—like it was all a great comic act that we were part of. David looked like he was in his element.

I was nervous. In his pre-match address Tubo didn't implore us to find our primitive selves nor did he lead us in prayer. There was quiet applause for us debutants. Someone hadn't turned up so I was going to start on the wing. There was the standard 'Let's go, Doggies' and we were through the door and into the day. Running. Side-to-side. Knees high without going anywhere. Some with footies taking nonchalant bounces like Darren Jarman. Then sprinting together en masse. By the second time round the centre square we were strung out over quite a bit of territory with a few of the boys sucking in the big ones. We stopped for a stretch. The skippers tossed. We walked to our positions. I shook hands with my opponent, a far more likable character than the Neanderthal at Strathpine. I was exactly where I wanted to be—on the wing for the Adelaide Lutheran seconds in the Adelaide Amateur Football League A6 reserves. I was playing footy.

The umpy looks around and gets the nod. David is in the centre. He is bent over like Mark Bairstow, hands holding the bottom of his shorts. Then he claps. He says something which I can't hear. The umpy holds the ball aloft. This is going to be a great season.

The siren sounds and the footy is thrown into the air. Our ruckman smashes it forward towards me and David and I converge on it. As David runs onto it the footy sits up on the hard centre wicket area and bounces towards me. I go to take it on the half volley and my opponent tries to kick it off the ground. He misses the ball but collects my hand. I still take possession of the footy but as my momentum carries me forward I know I'm in trouble. My finger is probably dislocated. I am tackled by about four opponents and have no chance of getting rid of the ball. The nervous umpire responds to the cry of 'Ball' from the nineteen-year-old mother-of-one standing on the boundary. I have given away a free kick.

I look at my skewiff finger. It feels like a dislocation. I stand the mark and put my good hand in the air. I have had a stack of dislocations over the years so when the trainer comes out I say, 'Brooksy, just put it back in will yuh? I'll be right.'

He can't. He pulls and I wince. He pulls again—hard. It kills. It really kills. He pulls again. 'Jeez, Brooksy, just pull on it.'

He puts some force behind it but he can't feel anything. I can. He is actually pulling on a broken finger; a finger where the tendon has been stripped from the top and bottom; a finger which is effectively only still connected by the skin. It just hangs there. 'You better come off,' he says.

By this stage I am in a lot of pain. I jog to the dressing room and as I go around the corner I slip on the concrete and hit the deck. I pick myself up and sit there in the dark. I am alone. I am wondering what to do. I realise I have a pretty serious injury and that I should see a doctor. I can hear the shouts of footy outside. I hear the calls. I hear the 'Harmsy, Harmsy, Harmsy,' and the 'Knock it back, knock it back' and the umpy's whistle. I hear the applause, the toots of the horn and the 'C'arn Doggies. 'Nother one, Doggies. Pile it on.' I hear all of this and it makes it worse. And I still don't know what I should do.

It's lucky we're playing lower grades footy because five minutes later a skinny young kid from Campbelltown–Magill accidentally runs into the point post and opens his forehead up. He needs stitches. He needs to go to hospital. They bring him to the dressing room next door. I come out to see what's happening. I hear one of the supporters saying they are going to take him up to casualty. I walk over, 'Excuse me, mate. Do you reckon I could get a lift up with you?'

'Oh yeah. I suppose. We're going now. Right now.'

I don't have time to tell anyone that I'm off to hospital. I am in the back seat of an HG Kingswood. In the front is a bloke with a towel pushed up against his eyebrow. I don't speak. The footy ground disappears from view.

At Modbury hospital I don't even have to sit in the crowded waiting room. I thank the bloke from Campbelltown–Magill for running into the point post and he sits in one of the plastic chairs while I'm rushed off on a trolley. They give me an injection. I go to X-ray. A nice woman takes off my footy boots and cuts the tape off my ankles. She asks me if I've eaten anything in the last twenty-four hours. I wonder whether a kilo and a half of capricciosa and half a dozen stubbies counts. A surgeon comes and tells me the finger is a big mess but they will see whether they can put it back together. I sign various documents. I want to request that my liver goes to a Bundy drinker where it will feel at home.

By three-quarter time I am on an operating table. A very junior anaesthetist is trying to deaden my left arm. I feel like deadening his. I am a human pin cushion. He and his offsider keep sticking their needle into a spot under my collarbone. He has about twenty-six goes at it. Nothing happens. The surgeon comes in and says, 'What are you doing?'

They look at him sheepishly. He waves his hand, 'Just knock him out.'

The next thing I remember is waking up in the ward. I am lying down but my hand is in a gallows sling. It is all wrapped up and connected to a metal stand. I have no idea of the time. I am in a lot of pain. I get a jab in the leg and fall asleep.

I wake up. No one in the world knows where I am. I find out I have had two and a half hours of micro-surgery. The surgeon has made a little incision and has wired my bones and tendons back together. I have had a five-second football season.

I ring David. The boys have won. David is half amused by my story. In truth he's very amused but he's pretending to be only half amused. He is amused because I am. I am amused because it's the only way I can deal with it. They come and pick me up.

Three weeks later I go back to hospital to get the stitches out. I have imagined about eight stitches. When my finger comes out of the bandages and the half-plaster it looks like a bratwurst. It is so swollen that the stitches are about five millimetres into the finger. And there aren't eight stitches—there are thirty-four. My finger has been completely reconstructed. And it will not bend at all.

Footy was out of the question.

The weeks went by. While the boys went off to training I visited the clinic at the Royal Adelaide where Naomi the physio held my hand. She had a device which measured the angle of flexion of my finger. We tried to improve its movement by one degree per visit and after a couple of months I could almost make a fist.

I stuck with the footy club. Sometimes I was Fos's runner. Adelaide Lutheran did pretty well, particularly against the sides where the threat of imminent death was not a factor in the outcome. There is a general rule in Adelaide footy that teams north and west of Gepps Cross are full of blokes who tend not to make the Sherrin the principal focus of the game. They tend to barrack for Port Adelaide. They tend to own pit-bull terriers. They tend to look like they've slept on a wet comic. They tend to get angry when a pooncy Lutheran gets past them with a simple blind turn.

One day at Ferryden Park, David played in the firsts. I was the runner. Adelaide Lutheran started strongly and the home side looked a little worried. They went the biff. The ball is in a scrimmage in the centre. It is kicked way out onto the vacant flank. David runs with the flight of the footy. His opponent is ten metres behind. David can't make the ball on the full. It lands on its point and bounces straight back over his head. He turns to chase it. As he turns his opponent, on the run, punches him right in the face. David is upended. I am about thirty metres away. In the few seconds it takes to get to him his eye is the size of a ping-pong ball with a little slit in it. He is very groggy. His legs don't work. We carry him off. We put him on the rub-down table in the dressing sheds and he starts to come round. The first thing he says is

'What won race four at Morphettville?'

Adelaide Lutheran played some excellent footy. In the match against Mitcham at Hawthorn we kicked ten goals into the wind in the first quarter. It was a majestic performance. We videoed that game and I commentated from the top of the toilet block.

The club was full of committed blokes. Chris Jahnke was an amateur league version of Tim Watson. He didn't quite have the Essendon champion's skills but he had his physique. He was the quintessential *bustling* ruck-rover. He hurtled himself around the paddock knocking over whatever got into his path. That sometimes included team-mates.

Nathan Zweck was studying medicine. He had a big moustache and plenty of skill and was able to lift those around him. Paul Kidney could just get the ball. So could Mark Schubert. Then there were the old warhorses like Koopy and Groeckes, and Ev Leske who taught ancient history and wore long sleeves, and the Krieg brothers who looked like a couple of the Bee Gees. Rod Rocket Ellis was in the state cricket squad. Bird Borgas and Sarge Schultz were studying for the ministry.

Munch was a star. He had tremendous poise, and a real footy brain. We needed blokes of his character at Geelong. So, too, Dudley Liebelt who held his own in the ruck despite being just over six foot. He had those Blu-tac hands and played with inspirational courage.

Our home ground was in the Parklands on Goodwood Road. That year it was wet and the ground didn't handle it too well. The dressing rooms were pretty basic. They were made of besser block, a material invented specifically for the footy dressing shed. There was tape everywhere, a collection of socks and other garments and a film of Adelaide Lutheran mud. By round fourteen everyone had developed the necessary immunities to the colonies of bacteria that thrived there. And it smelt like a good amateur league dressing room should.

These days things are different. Stolly is the president and Bongo is on the committee and the boys have built terrific club rooms with grand photos of those days in the mid-eighties when the club was starting out in the Amateurs. You can get a beer or a glass of Nat Zweck port to support his medical work in Africa. You can read the honour boards or have a countery—if Bongo and Janet have the kitchen opened.

Fos doesn't need a walking frame yet.

By the end of the year my finger was good enough to take part in the half time dob in the A-grade. Nothing improves a B-grade footballer like a pair of ug boots, some Levis, and a couple of beers. Blokes who couldn't get near the footy during the seconds would be flying for huge grabs and hitting blokes on the chest from forty-five metres. It's a fact of life.

The As finished fourth that year and the Bs lost in the preliminary final

The season's report said 'John Harms—one game.'

CHAPTER II

By the mid-eighties I had learnt that the Geelong Football Club had three types of season. There was the Make-the-Five-but-Lose-in-the-Preliminary-Final model (popular in the early eighties). There was the Finish-One-Game-out-of-the-Five model (popular throughout history). And there was the Season-Written-Off-by-Round-Eight model (of which 1975 was considered one of the classics). The design geniuses at Geelong, however, were working hard at developing a new model: the Get-Flogged-in-the-Grand-Final model (which was to become incredibly popular in the nineties).

The 1985 season was a classic example of the second model. We'd beat teams we weren't supposed to and lose to those at the bottom of the ladder. In round nine I was in Melbourne to see them play Richmond. I was very keen to see Gary Ablett live.

It was another freezing day at Waverley and the Cats were woeful. The game was woeful. And yet there was this hope that something would happen. Mark Jackson provided some comic relief. He and Greg Strachan traded blows for the entire first half. The goal umpire would race out like a policeman in a silent movie and warn them and then race back to the goal line. At one point Jacko landed a dozen successive blows to the Tiger full back's solar plexus. The goal umpire finally reported him. (During the week Strachan said that he hadn't been hit at all.)

The only highlight in the first three quarters was when a body appeared high above the pack about a hundred metres from where we were seated. It was Ablett. But even he couldn't inspire the Cats and at three-quarter time we had booted a whole 7.7 and were thirteen points behind. We were gone.

Disillusioned I went to get a couple of pies and a couple of cans for the troops. In the couple of minutes I was away Geelong had kicked two goals. They just went crazy, as if they had twice the number of players on the field. The Tiges were overrun. Mad Dog Morgan kicked four in the quarter. We kicked eleven altogether and won by fifty points. It was a momentous occasion: the first time I had ever seen Geelong win. From there it was win one–lose one and we ended up sixth again, a game and a half out of the five. There were plenty of these seasons during the eighties.

After my year in Adelaide I was employed as a teacher in a Brisbane secondary school. My teaching duties included quite a few PE classes. When Geelong won on Saturday I would wear my Geelong jumper to school on the Monday, and in 1986 I got to wear it all of seven times.

Things improved in 1987. For a start footy was coming to Brisbane. I had to pinch myself. My footy side was coming to me! The Cats would be playing in Queensland.

That year there were plenty of Mondays when I could don the Geelong jumper. We were starting to play some good footy—spectacular footy. Young talented blokes like Paul Couch and Mark Bairstow, Barry Stoneham and Billy Brownless were starting to have an impact. And, of course, there was Gary Ablett. I loved him. He made me feel like no other footballer ever. There were footballers, and then there was Gary Ablett. I didn't think too much about it. I just loved watching him.

At this time Geelong was one of those nuisance sides. Other supporters could never treat us lightly because they didn't know what to expect. Geelong supporters didn't know what to expect. The coach, John Devine, didn't know what to expect. It was as if it were all in the lap of the gods. We were a team which on our day could beat anyone in the competition. Not just beat them: make them look second rate. Then there'd be other days when we'd be 9.3 at the twenty-two-minute mark of the first quarter and lose by sixteen points—to St Kilda.

I didn't want to be part of a team which was a nuisance side. I wanted consistency. I wanted to know that when we played Fitzroy at home we would just win, and win like an odds-on favourite should. At times we were appalling. Not just bad, but break-your-heart appalling.

At least now we could see the Cats here in Queensland. I would often drive down to watch Brisbane play at Carrara. It was very weird to head to the Gold Coast to watch a game of VFL footy—to watch a platoon of football mercenaries play the tribes of Melbourne. The Bears looked like they were going to be the easy-beats of the competition. Even their coach, Peter Knights, was realistic about the squad he had and its chances.

Of course the very generous Geelong Football Club did everything in its power to make this new side welcome. We let the Bears flog us at Kardinia Park in round two. It was the sort of defeat that has Cats supporters punching walls and wondering what we've done to deserve a team like Geelong. Not another year like this!

Brisbane's first home game wasn't until round four, against Fitzroy. I drove down early and parked in the big grass paddock. It was one of those brilliant Queensland autumn days: cloudless, mid-twenties, a gentle breeze up the Nerang River. The oval looked in great nick, but the venue didn't have the feel of VFL footy as I remembered it. There was a fair-sized crowd in, though. I stood in the outer on the mound on the half-forward flank. It was like being on the hill at the Gabba. Around me were a whole stack of Fitzroy supporters, mainly blokes. They had decided to organise their annual holiday around their team's match on the Gold Coast. They had Fitzroy in their blood; they had footy in their blood. Most of them wore very tight Levis and sleeveless Fitzroy jumpers with 29 or 9 or 12 on their backs. There was a gallery of facial hair. They were ratbag blokes having a great time, telling funny stories about what had happened at some pub the night before. They were well on the way. The cans were going down beautifully.

It was to be a Brisbane Bears extravaganza; a Skase-inspired launch of ceremonial significance. Close to where we were standing was the truck which was to be used as the stage at half time. It was parked in the gateway where the ground staff would normally bring their equipment onto the field. The truck's cabin was obscuring a section of the forward pocket about the size of a beach towel. The ball was unlikely to run over the boundary line in that spot once in a whole season. Not long into the first quarter one Fitzroy bloke yelled out, 'Hey, Robbo. These idiots don't know how to organise football.' He nodded his head towards the truck. 'Can't see the oval, mate. Can't see it.'

As the Bears fumbled away on the field the Fitzroy boys started to chant: 'Shift the fucking truck. Shift the fucking truck.' Fitzroy kicked a few goals. They cheered. The chant resumed: 'Shift the fucking truck. Shift the fucking truck.' One of the blokes editorialised: 'There's just no consideration for the football public these days. No consideration of the punters.' He yelled out to the security zombie, 'Shift the fuckin' truck.'

The zombie yelled back: 'Why?'

The Royboy put his hands on his hips. 'Because we can't see the footy.'

In time-on the chant started up again: 'Shift the fucking truck.' The boys were looking a bit aggro and the zombie was starting to worry. He got on his walkie-talkie, 'We've got a problem here. Some of the patrons can't see the oval. Can you send someone over to shift the truck?'

The chant kept going. A bloke in King Gees saun-tered over looking bemused and the Royboys got very excited. Not only was their team leading by six goals at quarter time but they were clearly having an impact. They continued: 'Shift the fucking truck. Shift the fucking truck.'

The guy started up the motor and moved the truck back about four metres at which point, without missing a beat, the crowd started chanting: 'Bring back the fucking truck. Bring back the fucking truck.'

As the season progressed Geelong was settled in the five and looked like being competitive in the finals. Ablett had been brilliant but was suspended. He was returning for the Geelong match at Carrara. The Bears were languishing at the bottom of the ladder. Ablett's frustrations with Geelong's coach, John Devine, were well documented, and on this occasion Ablett was going to have to come back through the seconds as was the policy at the club. I wasn't too impressed, but that's the way it was.

I drove down to Carrara mid-afternoon. I still found it hard to believe that here I was heading off to the Gold Coast to see my beloved Geelong play VFL footy against Brisbane. I would be there in time for the seconds: in time to see the Great Man. Some friends would come down later.

When I arrived there was nobody around. The gates were still locked. The seconds were playing in Brisbane. I sat at the gate for two hours.

A bitterly disappointed Geelong supporter in a state of upset should never be left alone. He should not be allowed to wallow in the gangrene of his melancholy. He should not be able to pick at the scabs of his unsatisfied existence. It was a long two hours until I was discovered by the others. By that stage I had deduced that I was perversely drawn to the tragedy of the Geelong Football Club. My life was just a reflection of the team; a team I inexplicably continued to love. I fondled the swollen knuckle of my old football injury. It was cold and the wire holding it together was making it ache. Things just didn't work out when you barracked for the Cats.

At least I'd see the seniors. But it got worse. From the opening bounce it looked like we were in trouble. Brisbane thrashed us by about eight goals. I felt crook. I felt betrayed. We are being talked about as a serious finals contender and the boys come up to the coast and show absolutely no heart whatsoever. Geelong: they pissed me off.

We lost a couple more over the next month and suddenly we were in trouble. We had to win two of the last three to get in. The draw wasn't kind. We played the top three sides. Carlton hammered us in round twenty, and it looked like the end. The following Sunday I drove to Carrara to see the Brisbane–Footscray game. I had the trannie with me to get the scores of Geelong's clash against Tom Hafey's Swans. The Swans in Sydney: almost impossible. At half time we were down by four goals. We were going to miss out again. I stood in the outer watching a very ordinary game of footy waiting for the progress scores to break into the rugby league commentary. The Brisbane Bears were pathetic.

On the drive home I am trudging along at about eighty in my old '74 Corona. Again, I'm by myself. I hate footy. I hate how you always feel so let down; so defeated. I consider how bad the Bears were that afternoon. I wonder how they had beaten Geelong earlier in the season. I wonder why I bother? Why aren't I on the golf course or at some pub having a few lazy Sunday afternoon ales or at the movies? Why do I do it? Why do I put myself in a position of being let down?

One hand steers, the other plays with the knobs on the radio. The sun has just set which means I'm a chance of picking up some obscure Riverina station which will have the VFL on. Around Helensvale I hear the unmistakable chant of footy commentary. There's a lot of interference. For once the reception improves. The Cats are six goals down in the last quarter. But we're coming back. That'd be right—there isn't a Swans player in the call. We kick a couple. Maybe? We're storming home. We keep missing. Behind after behind, about five in a row. The Swans have got nothing left. Kick straight you idiots. Then a steadier for the Swans. It's over. The Cats get another one. I'm in the right lane. And another one. I'm in the right lane again. I decide to stay in the right lane. The traffic banks up behind me but I have a higher calling. The Cats get another one: that's three in a couple of minutes. And from the ball-up the ball falls to Lindner on the fly. He throws it onto his boot. It's a prodigious kick; a seventy-metre torp. It's through. The Cats have hit the front. I toot the horn. They get another one. I toot again. The Cats are home. Yes. Yes. The Cats: they're brilliant. Bruce Lindner, I love you. The final siren. We've kicked 8.8 in the last quarter to win.

I've done it. I've got them home. I've kept a fearless

and steady line in the right-hand lane of the Pacific Highway between Pimpama and Yatala and I've got the boys home. We're in the five. We can beat the reigning premiers next week. We can beat the second top side and stay in the five. Look out Hawks: you are in big trouble. When we make the five there'll be a few worried coaches. We're the wildcard. We can do some damage in this finals series. Geelong, I love you. You are one of the great sporting teams on this planet. And footy, there just isn't a game like it.

The next week I assume the game will be telecast on Channel 7. Geelong is in the five. Hawthorn is second. The game has got to be on telly. It's not. They show top-placed Carlton and fourth-placed North. Typical. It always happens. But there is a lot of interest in the Geelong–Hawthorn game and they give scores throughout the afternoon. The half-time highlights suggest Geelong is in control everywhere except on the scoreboard. At three-quarter time we lead by three goals. But we've killed them around the ground. We've kicked 13.15. They've hardly had the ball in their forward line. It's a great last quarter. I hang on every score. We stay on top. With a minute to go we're nine points clear. We're home. Jason Dunstall kicks two goals in the last thirty seconds. We're beaten by three points. We finish half a game out of the five. We don't know how to win.

It's too much.

CHAPTER 12

If ever a season opened with hope it was 1989. We had talent to burn. Experience. Youth. Vitality. Flair. And a new coach. Malcolm Blight was an inspired choice, a man who understood sheer brilliance. This was the year.

We lost the first game to North by two points.

The Ablett legend continued to grow. It was hard to know what position he played. He just sort of roamed around the ground winning kicks and then occasionally he'd go up forward and fly for a few marks, wrestle with his opponent, make a few leads—and kick eleven goals. I have a memory of him playing at Carrara, hovering miles in the air, above the stands, without having used an opponent to get there. He just jumped.

In the game against Collingwood he kicked seven. It was tight into the last quarter when Gazza just took over. He flew for marks at centre half forward and roved the very pack he'd just been part of. He kicked four in one of the most explosive twenty minutes of footy ever witnessed and all of Geelong—the players, the town, the supporters in lounge rooms around the country—were not just glad he was on our side, we were thrilled. Fair dinkum thrilled. Glad-to-be-alive thrilled.

He led the Geelong charge, but not the way of a conventional leader. He didn't pat players on the back and encourage them. He was just G. Ablett and he was one of the main reasons we thrashed some of the finals contenders. We held Melbourne to just a couple of goals and as the home and away season ended we looked like being a force in the finals.

On the Sunday of the qualifying final I organised a barbecue. I was in high spirits—briefly. We lost to Essendon by seventy-six points. It was another case of the Cats doing everything in their power to drive their supporters insane. But, in another great turnaround, we beat them by ninety-four points in the preliminary final two weeks later.

Not so long ago I met a bloke called John Dunne who now owns a bookshop in Geelong. He used to call the footy with the late Ted Whitten and the gang at K-Rock. Chatting over a couple of beers we realised that we were on precisely the same Geelong wavelength. We knew what it meant to be a Geelong supporter, and an Ablett-lover, and we sat reliving great Geelong moments. I went straight to the 1989 preliminary final. He just kept saying: 'I know. I know. I know what you're going to say.' And would recall the precise incidents which make that game so memorable. There were many.

It is a glorious spring day. Waverley is radiant green in the sunshine. The crowd is white with T-shirts and floppy hats. Conditions are perfect. Geelong play fast, clean open footy; as good a footy as you can imagine. They move the ball so quickly and with such skill that players seem to have more space. They are sensational. In one passage of play the ball comes out of the backline and Bourke marks. He turns and runs on and boots it towards Ablett who is bursting up the flank. Ablett marks in front of his face, seventy metres out from goal. He goes back quickly. Hamilton is on the mark. He looks like he's going to roost it forward. He fakes Hamilton, runs around him, sprints away and puts the footy through the middle, post high from fifty-five metres. Later in the game Hamilton takes possession of the footy and is about to clear from centre half back when Ablett swoops. In the instant between Hamilton dropping the ball and it hitting his boot Ablett has picked it out of the air and absconded. This is sheer joy.

The boys are brilliant. We will play Hawthorn in the grand final.

The 1989 grand final is much remembered, and much revered, by footy people everywhere. I wouldn't go a year without seeing it. I usually watch it before the start of each season and will return to it following some moment of great disappointment, late at night after Geelong has been thrashed in a night game at Footy Park.

The tape now flickers and jerks and jumps. It's getting to be like one of those favourite old T-shirts.

I remember the day. I am up at five. I have to go to Warwick where I am taking interschool tennis. It finishes on time and, as I fly through Cunningham's Gap, I think about the match. We can win this. If we can make it a fast, clean, open game it's ours. I get back home just as the Geelong reserves lose by a kick.

I watch it in the lounge room. The noise builds as the Geelong team come up the race. They gather behind the banner which says 'The Charge of the Blight Brigade'. It's such an important occasion that the Geelong cheer squad haven't risked poetry. They have drawn a horse, though, which looks like the sort you drew in grade three, with a Blight likeness perched on top. It's a noteworthy acknowledgment: Blight is the saviour-figure.

Hawthorn run through their banner which says, 'Well hello…Hawthorn. It's so nice to have you back where you belong.' It refers to this being the Hawks' seventh successive grand final appearance—they are the defending champions.

The teams jog around eyeing each other off before

settling and doing some stretching. The Cats look composed. They look ready. I feel good. Peter McKenna says it's going to be a great clash between the old campaigners and the young guns, 'between the dependable Hawks and the brilliant Cats.' The Hawks look like they belong, as if the premiership is rightfully theirs and it's simply a matter of dealing with the nonsense that Geelong think they have some claim to it.

Johnny Farnham sings the national anthem with the deaf children. The camera shows the crowd in the sunshine: kids with painted faces, bushies in Akubras, young women in footy guernseys. There is a lot of blue and white. Damian Bourke wins the toss and there is a roar.

Brereton struts around. Ayres is close by. They look like those caricatures that budding teenage artists used to send in to 'World of Sport': enormous heads with manes of hair, barrel chests and skinny legs. Chris Mew. Michael Tuck looking like something out of a McCubbin painting. Jason Dunstall rubbing turf between his palms. Johnny Platten chatting to Greg Dear.

The Cats are in the tightest huddle seen at the MCG for many years. Bourke speaks to them. They affirm their commitment. The huddle breaks and the noise grows. Ablett goes towards the square. His face is expressionless. Maginness picks him up. Jeans is kidding isn't he? The young Hawk looks concerned. Hamilton and Flanigan trot towards the bench. Schulze goes to Brereton. Buckenara starting wide on a wing. Lindner goes to him. Darcy's got Dunstall. Bruns on Dipierdomenico. Bourke, Bews, Couch and Hocking start in the middle. Tuck finds Bairstow up forward.

I have waited twenty-seven years for this. So have many at the MCG. Louder. Still louder. As umpire Peter Carey holds the ball aloft. Siren.

Carey thumps it into the turf and it bounces heavenward. Bourke and Dear leap at each other. Bodies come from everywhere and in the mad rush Bews grabs the footy and throws it onto his boot. Ablett is leading straight out from goal like a train. He marks.

Something's happened back in the middle. Brereton's down. He's on his back with his knees flexed. He holds his midriff and grimaces and stamps his feet. Ablett goals from outside the fifty. The footy sails through half-post high. Brilliant.

The producers locate the footage of the incident back in the centre. As the trainers lend assistance to Brereton we see the replay. Brereton and Schulze have run from centre half forward towards the centre. Mark Yeates has come from the wing and has charged straight at Brereton. They are well off the ball. Brereton is so focused on the play that, for once, he doesn't notice his tormentor coming. Yeates crashes into his ribs. The momentum of the collision sends Brereton's limbs out of control. His arms flail; his leg swings up and he hits the deck. As he is sprawled on the ground Yeates stands over him. There is purpose in his eyes; it looks like

Yeates is preparing to have another go. He steps towards Brereton but the replay stops. What happened? Why don't they show the next moments? Why has that footage never been shown? Is that when Brereton was really injured? I want to know. I have never liked Brereton and I kind of like it that Yeates has run through him, but something feels wrong.

In an instant all sense of fun and play disappear from the match. This isn't how I like footy. This isn't Geelong. The game is frenzied. There are bodies running everywhere. Brereton stays on. He limps to the forward pocket where Stephen Hocking picks him up. Dunstall marks and goals. Then Brereton marks above his head. It is as brave a thing as you will see on a footy field. There are little spot fires around the ground. On the wing Bews, Bruns and Hocking take on Dipper who holds his own while support arrives.

Then Brereton crunches Darcy who finishes up in the gutter. Stephen Hocking comes in to remonstrate. They wrestle. Brereton grabs his windpipe—so tightly that his fingers are nearly joined behind it. He's not kidding. He'll crush it if he can. This is not theatre. The younger Hocking throws himself around. He hits Kennedy late. Free down the ground. Goal. He hits Dipper late. Goal. He clashes with Platten. Platten doesn't return to the game. What is happening here? This isn't how we play. We're not barbarians, head-hunters; we're footballers. Hawthorn make the most of this lack of discipline; this stupidity. The Hawks go four goals up and we look gone. This is terrible. And we deserve it.

Hawthorn also show their strength. They won't be bullied. Ayres shirt-fronts Ablett who goes down. It is a blow that would stop a charging bull, but Ablett gets up and shakes his head and sets off. Minutes later he is late to a contest. Dipper stands under the ball on the half back flank. Ablett flies into his back. It is crude; a less than generous action indicative of the Geelong spirit of the first quarter. Although he doesn't know it at the time, Dipper has broken ribs. He plays the rest of the game.

The Hawks are superb. Bairstow gets clear inside fifty but Tuck comes from nowhere to mow down his direct opponent. Hocking fumbles like the guilty schoolboy who's looking over his shoulder waiting for the square-up and Buckenara pounces and goals. Right is with Hawthorn—and I know it. Lindner takes a great mark at half back but is called to play on, is dispossessed and Brereton marks in the square. Hawthorn lead by six goals. The siren sounds. I shake my head. Is this what we've waited for? What has entered the minds of these men? Who are these Geelong players? I am not upset because we're down, I'm upset because we've had so little faith in our footy skills that we've resorted to violence. This is not the team I love. I can't even work out whether I want them to win or not.

We try hard to work our way back into the game in the second quarter. At least we settle down. Flanigan gives some drive in the ruck and around the ground. Lindner looks like he still believes he can make his side win. And Shane Hamilton keeps getting free. Perhaps the Hawks haven't given him the respect he deserves. Couchy gets a few telling touches. Maybe.

The ball moves quickly. Ablett is one out with Maginness. They tussle. At the last instant, as the ball seems to have gone over their heads, Ablett pushes away from the contest. He dives back, throws out his paw—out, above, and behind—and drags in the mark with one hand. From the dead pocket he banana-kicks. The Basil Fawlty goal umpire signals a goal. Deep down he wants to drop his flags and stand there and applaud.

Every time we get a bit closer Hawthorn make the most of a half chance. Pritchard is terrific. Dunstall makes two team-lifting tackles: one on Bews which results in a goal. We keep coming. Hamilton finds Ablett on a fierce lead and he marks in front of his face. His third goal.

There is a boundary throw-in deep in Geelong's congested forward pocket. Hawthorn push back. A pack of players mills around as Dear and Flanigan jostle in the ruck. Ablett comes over the back, gets the ride, plucks the ball from way above them, lands, and off one step snaps high. Goal.

The tone of the game has changed. It's as if all of the levels have been established and the game will now be played within them. The level of physical pressure remains high but the contest has lost much of its smelly brutality. The footy is swept from end to end. The Cats put together chains of handballs. But Mew saves the day. But Collins clears. But Pritchard intercepts. Geelong are becoming the instigators, Hawthorn the reactors. Yet the Hawks take every chance and deserve their lead at half time: 12.9.81 to 7.2.44.

The Cats come out determined to make the third quarter theirs. Hawthorn brace themselves. Langford goes onto Ablett. Lindner understands the reality of 'now'. He displays real footy instinct. He backs himself picking up in traffic, blind-turning and creating opportunity. Yeates takes a screamer. Flanigan backs into a pack and marks. He hits the post. Ablett takes a beauty in front of goals and kicks truly. There are the slightest cracks appearing in the Hawthorn fortress. Mew won't leave Stoneham's side. Ayres hears Ablett's footsteps bearing down on him and drops an easy mark. It is one of the few errors he makes in his career.

Geelong are taking risks, pushing forward. Hocking dodges. The skills are remarkable. Hamilton picks up at full pace and gives a diving handball to Couch who sends a long bomb to Brownless. He's got it. He kicks a point. The Cats are everywhere. They seem to be winning the tight contests. They run and run. Stoneham wins the ball and gets it to Malakelis who puts it into the path of Ablett. The ball is now the focus. Scott watches it so intently that he chips in front of Ablett and marks thirty metres out. He kicks a point.

We're twenty-two points down and just when Hawthorn have the wobbles, Anderson makes something from nothing. He gathers the ball near the boundary and throws it onto his left foot. He has kicked it towards the square but it floats. It doesn't spin. And through it goes. They needed that.

Players take possession of the footy and fire out authoritative handballs which open up great sweeps of play. Lindner rockets one to Bairstow on the fly. He pins his ears back and streams through the centre. This is footy. He rockets a pass to Brownless who marks. Billy looks apprehensive. He goes to lay off. The crowd scream at him, 'Just go back and put it through Billy!' So do his team-mates. From fifty-five metres he does.

But we don't know how to win. Darcy jumps on Dunstall and gives away fifty and then Bewsy makes a mistake and Buckenara takes advantage and if only we believed in ourselves a bit more. Suddenly, despite the flow of the game the Hawks are forty-three points up again. It doesn't look like that sort of game though.

Ablett uses Kennedy as a stepladder and takes a screamer. The crowd shake their heads. How much talent does this man have? He kicks his sixth. There is still no expression from the Great Man. It falls to him again and he snaps with his left. This will bring the house down. He misses by about a metre. Then Hamilton bounces one through on the siren and we're still thirty-six points down.

What will make the Geelong team believe they can

still win this game? There's a sense around the stadium that it's not over yet. Do the Geelong players believe it? The Hawks have been pummelled. Platten hasn't returned—and won't. Brereton has been brave but must be struggling. There is more pressure to absorb. I am hopeful.

It gets worse for Hawthorn. In the opening minutes of the last quarter Tuck splits the webbing on his hand. He calls for help. Geelong go forward but Langford stands his ground and takes a great mark in front of Ablett. Bruns goals but Buckenara replies within thirty seconds. Then Flanigan goals for Geelong. Then Ablett. Mark. Goal. There's a chance. We go forward again but Langford stands tall for another saving mark. A streaker flashes past: a woman in a black cape. It is the sort of game where she is given nothing more than a cursory glance. Couch gets caught and the ball spills to Wittman who finds Dunstall. 'No!' Goal. Another Geelong mistake.

Stoneham beats Mew and goals and the Hawks look out on their feet. The formal structures which have held them together are almost obliterated. They stand doubled over trying to find something. The Cats are really coming now. Lindner gathers at half back. He gets through the trouble, he fakes, and he's into the daylight. He's clear. He bounces. He bounces again. We know where it's going. Long to Ablett, one out with Langford. They're locked together. Time slows. We wait. Ablett can't take the mark. He can't pull it in with his left hand. It bounces once. Ablett recovers. Gathers. Two steps. Perfect balance. Left foot snap. Goal. It's a goal. Ablett.

The Cats go forward again. Ablett flies. Hamilton roves. He steadies. Snaps. He pumps the air. It's another one. Eleven points the difference. Ten minutes to go. The Hawks are in trouble. There are tears in the crowd. This is too much. People are alive. They chant 'Gee-*long* clap-clap-clap. Gee-*long* clap-clap-clap.' They look at each other. Could they?

Hawthorn scrap. They will not lie down. They push the ball forward and it falls to Anderson who goals. They're still making the most of their chances. They encourage each other. Those who can are doing the work: Pritchard, Collins, Mew, Condon, Anderson. You can feel their effort.

But the Cats are relentless. They surge forward. The ground is getting bigger. There is more space; more opportunity if you can find the strength to run. The Cats believe. Six minutes to go and Scott has a chance. He misses. Seventeen points. The Hawthorn supporters won't give the ball back. They're making their contribution. A policeman goes after it. It provides precious recovery time as the ball is retrieved. Langford kicks out and the game flows again. It's desperate. Some take their chances. Others waste them. End to end. How can they keep going? Geelong go forward. High to Ablett in the square. Yeah. He marks it overhead. It's one of those moments when outstretched arms appear in front of the cameras as people have leapt from their seats in unison. They scream, 'Yes. Yes.' Ablett kicks his ninth. Eleven points. There's time. There's time. There's enough time. There is. There is.

The Hawks will not give in. Every player is searching for something; some last reserve to permit a last effort. Curran kicks a point and it's twelve points the difference. There's a mad scramble. Players throw themselves at the footy. The Hawks try to bottle it up. But it comes free. Wide to Hamilton. On to Scott. The Cats are away. Loose men everywhere. Cameron. Fifty metres out directly in front. A minute to go. 'Kick it. Go back and kick,' I yell in the lounge room. 'Too slow. Too slow,' they yell in the crowd. Cameron goes back and puts it through. There are forty seconds left.

At the centre bounce players come from everywhere. We've got to get it out of the centre. Please. There's a second ball-up and the tap falls to Bewsy. A chance. He goes to kick. And fakes. Like he has all day. And he's caught. And there's about to be another ball-up when the siren goes. The crowd screams. Hawthorn have won.

I am pumped and floored at the same time. I burst through the french doors which fling backwards more quickly than I anticipate and the handle puts a hole in the fibro wall on the verandah. It remains there for four years, a constant reminder of the Geelong Football Club.

I watch the presentation. Malcolm Blight walks

among his deflated players. Ablett wins the Norm Smith Medal. He still has shown no emotion. His opponent in the second half, Chris Langford, has been one of Hawthorn's best—and Ablett has kicked five goals on him. Yet Langford has taken three steadfast marks, one where he has refused to allow the weight of the flying Ablett to carry him under the ball. It is one of the marks of the day: the resolute in the face of the spectacular.

Over the next few days I work out that in this drama Hawthorn is the hero, Geelong the villain. Good has triumphed. And the villain has learnt a moral lesson.

I am glad that Hawthorn won.

PART 3

The despair I can handle, it's the hope that kills me.
John Cleese

Some people are destined never to experience joy, satisfaction and fulfilment in their lives. For these people God has given us the Geelong Football Club.
Guru Bob of the Coodabeen Champions

CHAPTER 13

Some people believe that I am obsessed with the Geelong Football Club and that I watch the 1989 grand final far too often. I love Geelong but it has never been an obsession. It is a deeply meaningful passion. It has only *appeared* like an obsession. The reason for this is that friends and relatives—who have jobs and families, people who pay their taxes and put out their wheelie-bins and generally live normal lives— keep giving me Geelong paraphernalia. And they think *I've* got the problem.

They are the ones who have bought me Geelong stuff for Christmases and birthdays for twenty years. I have Geelong key rings, Geelong stubby-holders, a hand-knitted Geelong scarf, a hand-knitted Geelong tea-cosy, homemade Geelong shorts, a Geelong sunglasses case, a Geelong sports bag, a Geelong beach towel, a Geelong barbecue apron, Geelong wood-head covers, numerous Geelong T-shirts including one with Sylvester the Cat wearing a Geelong jersey, Geelong books, Geelong playing cards, Geelong stickers, Geelong gift-wrapping paper, a Geelong pullover, little Geelong men who sit in the kitchen window, little Geelong men who sit on the old radiogram, Geelong everything. They are all gifts. Do you think I'd buy this stuff?

And then there is the Ablett stuff. I admit I bought all the Ablett books because I am fascinated by him and I bought my own fair dinkum long-sleeved Geelong footy jumper. And I do have a cat called Ablett. But I didn't buy the Ablett fridge magnet, the Ablett posters, the Ablett jigsaw puzzle, or the T-shirt with a big picture of Ablett on it (which I sometimes forget I'm wearing when I pop down to the local TAB to put on a Moe treble).

I do, however, have an admission. In the early nineties I put together a basketball team which I called Geelong. I spent a whole weekend painting blue hoops on ten Bonds singlets and gave myself number 5. This single indulgence did generate some criticism. We played in the lowest grade and got a few laughs. And wouldn't you know it, in our first season we lost the grand final.

We had a significantly better season in 1990,

however, than the footy club we were named after. Despite the mammoth predictions which accompanied the grand final—that a new era had dawned at Geelong—the Cats struggled in 1990. We were going to be a new force under Malcolm Blight; a solid, dependable, flash but gritty team. Nothing came of the promises. In one match I nearly went crazy. We dominated the game against Carlton to such a degree that at half-time we led 9.17 to 4.6 and should have been twelve goals up—easily. We lost.

Geelong was a mystery. We had such a good team; such talent. We could turn it on. Why did this always happen? Why did we promise so much and deliver so little? Was this the calling of Geelong: to show people everywhere that there could be a greater purpose in suffering?

In 1990, Collingwood won the scrubbiest premiership in the history of the VFL, in a very scrubby season.

When I returned to uni to do an MA in Australian studies, I discovered that there was good writing about footy. I read Manning Clark's *Occasional Writings* which included an essay, 'At the Footy'. I discovered Garrie Hutchison's *From the Outer*. I could identify with Brian Matthews' joy in *Oval Dreams* as he stumbled around his warm kitchen during an Adelaide Hills winter watching footy. The things that footy meant to him also meant something to me. I could sense his love for the game, despite the frustration it caused him, and his appreciation of the players. I was given Ross Fitzgerald and Ken Spillman's excellent collection *The Greatest Game* for Christmas one year. The essayists and poets encouraged my belief that there was something in footy. Some of the writers I knew from their work in newspapers, like Martin Flanagan; some from studying history, like Geoffrey Blainey.

Footy was embraced by the intelligent and the thoughtful; those who had opened their hearts in their attempts to understand. I loved that Noel Counihan had shaken the hand of Cazaly and Picasso and that someone had thought that worthy of writing about. I laughed at Barry Dickins' perma-angst in *You'll Only Go in for Your Mates*, and was always happy to take the word of a man who praised Dunlop Volleys. His Fitzroy was my Geelong. I loved the poetry: especially Bruce Dawe's 'The High Mark' and his often quoted 'Life-Cycle'. This was my football world.

I went searching for other footy poetry and found that many fair dinkum, capital-P poets had written about footy in a way which suggested footy mattered; it really mattered. For weeks I sat in the uni library poring through poetry books until a librarian finally asked what I was doing and pointed me to a computer search. I found enough to write a paper on footy and Australian poetry. Poems by Gwen Harwood, Mark O'Connor, Barry Dickins, Peter Kocan and marvellous poems about the types of kicks by the late Philip

Hodgins who had another poem called 'Country Football'.

I was starting to wonder whether it was footy that grabbed me or the meanings it harboured.

It was football. And Gary Ablett. When he disappeared at the start of the 1991 season I was shattered. Why did these things happen? Why did they happen to Geelong? To me? And yet there was always the hope that he would return. He had too much footy left in him. A few rumours drifted north but it was hard to trust rumours which had made it beyond the Barassi Line. In Melbourne footballers have friends and family; they have conversations in video shops and petrol stations. In Brisbane in those days you had to try and piece things together yourself, or break the code of journalism-speak. G. Ablett was, to say the least, an enigmatic character.

Early that season Geelong came to Brisbane and on a sunny day at the Gabba kicked 27.28. Billy Brownless—the boy from Jerilderie—got a bag and the Cats looked very good. I couldn't say 'Billy Brownless' without saying 'the boy from Jerilderie.' He was like some cartoon character. It was as if someone decided to construct a player from the country and give him the most appropriate name in footy: Billy Brownless. He was the perfect Geelong recruit: tall, athletic, brilliant on his day, but about as reliable as rainfall on the Hay Plain.

Ablett did return and had there been a fatted calf in the back yard it would have been in grave danger. We won a stack in a row, strolled into the finals and would have been in the grand final if we hadn't done some really dumb things in the major semi against Hawthorn. We had them on the ropes—even without Ablett who was out suspended. We looked like running away with the game, only Sean Simpson kicked into the man on the mark when we were streaming forward to get that goal which would have, for once, broken them. It was a terrible turn-over and proved more than enough to trigger doubt of the Geelong variety and we went down by a whole two points. And it was also enough for us to get done by the Eagles in the preliminary final the following week.

More and more games were being shown on television. They were being scheduled across the weekend. We'd even get the occasional Friday night match—from about one in the morning. This meant a full media blackout—no news—for the night. All phone calls had to be answered with a very quick, 'G'day, don't tell me the score.' There were many times when I would sit up to watch the Cats in the middle of the night. I remember one game in Perth when the Eagles had hardly lost a match all year and we were looking to keep second spot and the double chance. Again we had them, until Stephen Hooper, the number one draft pick, dished out one of the worst handballs in human history and somehow the Eagles got back into it and won by a point.

It is probably a good thing that you can't see your-self watching footy on TV at three thirty in the morning. If you could you'd probably upgrade your health insurance and check into a clinic somewhere. You act strangely, occasionally jumping off the couch, the doona flying into the air. And you yell. Loudly. You don't mean to yell but the sublimely skilful Ken Hinkley (whom you love), a great backer of his own (outstanding) judgment leaves his opponent (which worries you because you lack faith) to make a contest on the wing. He flies, takes the grab brilliantly (which delights you), hits the ground running, turns into trouble (which infuriates you), beats one opponent with an exquisite dummy and another with a blind turn (which delights you even more), has a bounce and hits G. Ablett lace out forty from goal. Which makes you yell. That's precisely why God gave us the gift of yelling—because he knew he was going to give us Kenny Hinkley as well. And all this in a couple of seconds. Imagine being on this roller-coaster of mental ill health for a whole desperate one-goal-in-it quarter, a whole match, a whole season, a whole lifetime.

And Anthony William Brownless. Try not yelling at Billy in the middle of the night. The Cats are coming back. There's about ten minutes to go. We've kicked the last three. One more and we've hit the front. Ablett and Sean Wight are locked together in the goal square. Billy has the sit. He flies. He gets the ride. He is in textbook position: knee cocked on Gazza's shoulder, hands in front of his face. He's up there. He's done all the hard work. Ian Robertson yells, 'Brownless!' The footy slips through his hands and hits him in the scone. Of course you yell. '*NO, BILLY.*' There is no other possible response.

As he jogs away, Billy looks a little sheepish, hits his palm with his fist, and you can see him thinking, 'Oooh, probably should have marked that.'

We get done by a couple of points.

Not long after my thirtieth birthday (Geelong came from five goals behind St Kilda at three-quarter time to win by three points that afternoon and the evening's party was saved) I spent some time in Melbourne. I was thinking about doing a PhD down there. I went to check out the uni and a few golf courses and the weather and all those things that make life bearable.

I also wanted to get to Kardinia Park. I had never been. The Cats were going brilliantly in 1992. They were belting sides by putting together huge scores. I had seen them kick 37.17.239 against a woeful Bears at Carrara.

The week I was there we were playing the reigning premiers, Hawthorn. We had won ten of our previous eleven games and were premiership contenders. I caught the train to Geelong. It was full of supporters— lots of Hawthorn jumpers and Geelong flags. Down through Yarraville and Spotswood (which I had thought was a movie) and all those places. I read the *Age* and listened to the previews on my little radio. It was all there. You didn't have to hold the co-axial cable or ride down the street to get the special paper. This was what people did in Melbourne. It was what I could do every week if I lived here. You didn't have to fight for it. It was real, not imagined. I wondered whether that was what I wanted.

I get off with everyone at South Geelong. At the eastern gates the concession queue is very long. I have bought a ticket—there was an outside chance that this top-of-the-table clash would be sold out. A blackboard reads, 'Bass tickets here' but the gate isn't open. I mention this to a bloke in an official-looking smock who says he'll find out when it will be opened, then he thinks again and lets me through. I buy a *Record* and find a place on the terrace up the city end with people who've been coming to Kardinia Park all their lives; people whose grandparents went to the footy at Corio Oval; people who'd worked on the wharves and in the wool stores and at Pivot Fertiliser; people who read the *Addie*; people who buy their season's ticket before they get their toothache seen to; people whose life's work once filled the coffers of the Pyramid Building Society.

These are people who've put the nation's Ford motor vehicles together and people who've fed the people who've put the nation's Ford motor vehicles together. There are blokes who fought at El Alamein and know a good chicken chow mein. There are mothers of six and grandmothers of many more. They have their footy kit on: coats and gloves and beanies and badges and scarves and Geelong jumpers with numbers on the back. Number 5s everywhere. They live for Geelong.

It is one of those Victorian winter days when showers scud across from the south-west making recreational fishing inadvisable and footy miserable. Then it is sunny for a while and the glare off the wet grass makes it difficult to see and just as you're drying off a big cloud comes from nowhere and it gets black black and the wind picks up and it blows the rain sideways and into your face. And then the sun comes out again.

The seconds look OK. There are a few guys who show a bit: a fellow called John Barnes and another kid called Peter Riccardi. Ray Sterrett struggles. Who is in charge of recruiting at Geelong?

We wait for the seniors. I have a pie and a carton of chips. The Cats come out. What are these people thinking? Are they in the same state of battered uncertainty as I am? Are they telling themselves to be confident? Or are they more honest with themselves and admit they have absolutely no idea whether the boys have come to play today? There are a few voices: 'Go Gazza,' 'Go Billy,' 'Go Buddha.' The Hawks supporters colour the terrace like grey hairs in a young man's beard. They don't say much.

From the first bounce we are in trouble. The contest is almost all over by quarter time. We are broken. By half time some fans are upset, some are angry. I shake my head. It was always going to happen.

For a side that had been in sparkling form for weeks we play with horrible self-doubt. It is painful to watch. It is so magnificently in character. When Ablett marks twenty metres out and kicks a point a Hawks supporter finds voice: 'You're a Hawthorn reject, Ablett.'

Hawthorn is clinical. They wait on every Geelong error and then take the ball away with confidence and precision. I know what every Geelong supporter is thinking. We are all asking, why is our footy team like this? And of ourselves, why are we like this? Football is about inadequacy.

Ablett winds up at full back on Dunstall and we kick a few quick ones at the end to make the score less humiliating. It is an instructive afternoon. I couldn't live in Melbourne. I couldn't feel like this every Saturday afternoon.

On my return to Brisbane Geelong started winning again. We finished top that season and beat Footscray twice in the finals to make the grand final again, against the West Coast Eagles.

Grand finals are different. They seem to take longer. They're rougher. Match-ups can act as small contests which become the measure of what is happening. Personal duels. In 1992 the test case becomes Bairstow on Matera. If Bairstow can beat Matera, Geelong will win. We lead at half time but it doesn't look good. I ring David in Adelaide. 'We're gone,' he laments.

'We've used a lot of petrol for not much result.'

Brett Heady goes berserk and Blight is slow to react. As good as Couch has been in the first half Heady cuts him up in the third quarter. But there is still a chance. Bairstow tries his heart out. If he can get on top of Matera, maybe the Eagles will panic and the Cats will exploit their caution and build. Maybe. Bairstow gets twenty-five touches. So does Matera. But the young Eagle has been chosen. He runs at the ball and gathers it without breaking stride. His shots at goal sail through post high. When Bairstow has his chance in the early minutes of the last quarter he puts everything into his shot from forty metres. It is touched on the line.

Ablett has been spasmodically brilliant. But he is not at the centre of things. He has a supporting role. Blight has won a great following over four seasons but he hasn't understood this game. His players who played well on the day, players who count—Hinkley, Ablett, Barnes, Bairstow—haven't played roles that count. Brownless has been thrashed. The Cats have had their opportunities but we've been beaten. Defeated. The premiership cup leaves Victoria for the first time.

It takes Geelong to lose it.

CHAPTER 14

I needed to do something which assisted the plight of the Cats. If I were out of the country, Geelong was almost certain to win the flag. So, in the interests of the club, I decided to go on a big trip. I would visit Spud in London, travel around England and Scotland, take in some of the 1993 Ashes series, go to the British Open at Sandwich, and then backpack around Europe for six weeks. Spud, having eventually graduated in philosophy, had headed overseas—and was still there five years later. He had married a local, Jacqui, and was very happy. He was the general manager of a large handbag company—a useful man for a Geelong supporter to know. Despite my noble intentions I couldn't bring myself to stay away for the grand final. My ticket had me returning into Melbourne on the morning of the grand final—just in case.

Before I left I spent a couple of weeks in Adelaide. Eight years had passed since I'd lived there and the boys were all making their way in their respective professions. Stolly was a successful electrical engineer designing computerised cash registers for pubs and sports venues, David was working at one of the major hospitals and Bongo was developing new and improved shampoos for Davroe. They all had 150-game careers at Adelaide Lutheran behind them and had many yarns to tell. The club was very strong and in some seasons had fielded four sides.

I was still resting on the laurels of my five-second footy career. Every March I'd think about signing up for a season of footy in Brisbane. It never happened, but I still hoped to kick a goal in a fair dinkum fixture. It was one of my life's ambitions so David and Stolly and I hatched a plan. We would all play for the Cs: Stolly, stoic at full back, David, well below his grade in the centre and me on a half forward flank. It would be fun. We even talked Rocket into having a run.

We played Pulteney Old Scholars, a friendly side of blokes who knew the words to 'Three Little Maids from School' and were seriously thinking about buying a framed Allan Border portrait. Both sides ran a lot quicker with the footy than without it. I still had a bit of toe so it wasn't too difficult to get clear. Every time David got the footy he'd put it out in front of me on the big Adelaide Lutheran ground. Running into space is one of the joys of footy. For an instant it is as if there's only you and a footy and a patch of grass. It is pure freedom. And when you get the footy you've got room to move and time to do something. Whenever I got the ball I kicked high to Rocket at centre half forward.

At one point David took a mark about sixty out from goal. This was the chance. He waited until I dropped back into the square. I led into the pocket. He shook his head. It was the sort of footy where he could wait for me to get back to the square and make another lead. He beckoned me to come straight at him. I found a bit of space and marked, thirty-five metres out on the slightest of angles. This was it. I could hear Mick laughing on the boundary. I put the ball on the ground, pulled up my socks said to the bloke on the mark, 'This is one of my life's great moments.' He looked at me quizzically. My high drop punt came down over the top of the goalpost. The umpy ran across. Goal! David ran to me, laughing. I punched the air. It was a punch of delight and a punch of frustration. This could have been my 350th game. Still, I couldn't stop smiling, and I left it for people to work out for themselves how serious I was.

We ran out of legs at about the twelve-minute mark of the third quarter and Pulteney got the better of us. During the game one of their guys took one of those great speccies one-on-one in the centre, the type which appear on 'Almost Footy Legends'. We all stood around applauding.

The twenty-five-year history of the Adelaide Lutheran Football Club reads: 'John Harms 1985–93, games—2, goals—1.'

There was plenty to do in London. As I was off watching the cricket at Headingley and playing golf at St Andrews the Cats started clawing their way back into what had been another topsy-turvy season. In a phone call home I was told that Gary Ablett had taken the greatest mark of all time over Collingwood's Gary Pert. ('You cannot imagine how good this mark is. You just have to see it,' I was told.) We'd beaten Collingwood and flogged North Melbourne. We were a chance if we won every game.

I had always followed English soccer. Spud and I decided we'd go to the Charity Shield at Wembley, the day which marks the opening of the new soccer season. It is a sunny day. I am in a great mood. I have phoned home to learn that Geelong have thrashed Hawthorn by almost a hundred points. We are playing great footy.

Spud and I take the tube, which is crowded. There are Arsenal people everywhere. There are a few Manchester United fans and a lot of police as we walk with the stream of people along the huge walkway to the gate. The soccer louts have their shirts off. They have earrings, nose rings, all sorts of rings and a selection of allegiance-claiming tattoos. They walk with an aggressive swagger. It's best if you choose your moment to look at them. Generally, though, the mood is friendly. This is a fun day; a day which doesn't really count.

Spud and I walk up to the gate with a group of about a dozen of these lads. A throng of bobbies guard the entry. Of all the young men within twenty metres of the turnstiles I look most like a choir boy. Yet I am pulled out to be frisked. A policewoman and her offsider are about to give me the once-over. But she sees the absolute shock in my face and says, 'On your way.'

I know Wembley from TV. I've hardly missed an FA Cup in years. Wembley means something—like Cracker Night used to. The singing of 'Abide with Me' is one of the great moments in sport, but it's not simply about sport. I imagine the shared grief of those who attended the FA Cup final when the hymn was first sung in the years following World War I. Soccer was the joy amid the sadness; the affirmation of life.

The Charity Shield marks the new season by remembering the old: the FA Cup holders play the defenders of the league championship. Three performers led the crowd in 'Maybe It's Because I'm a Londoner' and the guvnor in the next row mouthed the words and shed a tear—and shed another during the national anthem. Then the chanting started. They all started together and remained in such perfect unison, speeding up together, getting louder together. It was amazing, but the soccer wasn't. It was dull: twenty blokes standing in a huddle around the centre of the ground seeing who could beat the offside trap. It was all very congested and lacked flow. As we walked back to the tube I was surprised at how civilised and friendly the whole afternoon was. I mentioned it to Spud. He said he'd take me to another sort of game.

Some months later, during my second overseas trip, Spud and I went to Stamford Bridge, Chelsea's home ground in London, to see them play Aston Villa. We came out of the station to be greeted by a scene which was quite sinister. All the way to the ground there were police in riot gear lined up shoulder to shoulder for several hundred metres. They held riot shields. Some police were on horseback. The horses wore special plastic goggles. Some police had clipboards and walkie-talkies. The cloud was heavy overhead. It was cold and dark.

There was an atmosphere of menace; a sense that the police were deployed for a reason and a threat that order could become chaos at any second. The scene made me think I was among angry people and, even worse, made me *feel* I was among angry people. I never felt this way at the footy in Australia. There could be a mood at Footy Park that a Crows' victory would appease but not necessarily satisfy, a parochial mean-spiritedness, but nothing like this. At home I was usually among happy and expectant people who yearned for glorious victory but understood defeat.

Losses sent us into ourselves to contemplate the nature of things, not into the street to growl and kick and punch and smash.

I went to the ticket office outside the ground, a little box with an old man in it. 'Two adults please?'

'You Chelsea then?' he asked.

'Not really. We're neutral.' I was honest, but naive.

'Well you can fuck off then. Go and sit with Villa.'

I told Spud the story. He got the tickets. We headed off for a pre-match beer. The Slug and Lettuce looked like it had been the scene of many a celebration and many a courage-lifting pint. 'Bohemian Rhapsody' filled the pub. Over and over. The boys in the corner were pumped. I felt like I was in a movie. Spud suggested that spontaneous friendliness could be interpreted the wrong way. I tried not to make eye contact with anyone, and certainly didn't say g'day.

Inside Stamford Bridge it all looked so old. The tiny wooden seats were very close together in the wooden grandstand. No one would have a chance in a fire. We sat with Chelsea fans who looked like Andy Capp. Almost all of them were men. If there were women around they were in a different part of the ground. Oddly, there were very few children. Australian footy is about children.

The crowd was the colour of winter overcoats and flat caps. There were only Chelsea scarves. The Villa supporters were corralled into a small area on the opposite side of the ground. No more than a thousand of them. They were noisy, attempting to make their presence felt, wanting to assert their loyalty.

The Chelsea fans found their voice as well. In the lead-up to the game there was to be a minute's silence in honour of the legendary Manchester United manager Matt Busby who had died during the week. The Chelsea fans in the Shed refused to maintain the silence. There is a sadness when a lone voice breaks the silence. It tells you why the world is as it is. And then another voice, encouraged by the first, rings out. And a couple more and you wonder why the comments are so malicious. Where does the hatred come from? I was reminded of one of their chants. 'How many lived and how many died in the Munich air disaster? Too many lived and not enough died in the Munich air disaster.'

It had been a tense day since arriving at the station. The match itself didn't show what a great game soccer can be. It finished in a one-all draw and the Chelsea fans went home disappointed. Even the sixty-somethings around us barked at the players and the ref. It was a grim afternoon.

Not long after the Charity Shield I went to Paris. I had six weeks to see a few things. By the time I got to the south of France the Cats needed to win their last two matches.

The village of Seguret outside Orange is so wonderful I can't leave. Only a handful of travellers are staying in the local hostel: Beth Gex, an American concert violist from Vienna; Chris, a writer from Los Angeles; Jan, a Dutch classical guitarist who has spent ten days on a pushbike to get to Seguret; two translators from Boulogne; a Geordie union official; Pete, who is a songwriter from Princeton and his beautiful travelling companion Arielle, an Oklahoman environmental science student. Each evening the owner cooks a five-course meal for us for about fifteen dollars and we sit at the long table under the tree in the courtyard. One night Beth plays for us: the 'Prelude and Allemande' from Bach's sixth solo suite. I cannot keep the tears from my eyes. We talk, really talk. These are intelligent and sensitive people.

It is also a happy time because I learn that Geelong has crushed the top side Essendon and, even though we're still outside the six with a tough game against West Coast in Perth in the final round, Peter tells me that the experts are talking the Cats up. He tells me that they're saying we're the best side in a very even competition. We're seventh, yet we're premiership favourites. This is so Geelong.

During the last week of the season I am in Florence with Beth. We eat lunch and drink wine and go to the Academia. We see David, but it is Michelangelo's unfinished sculptures which really grab me. It's as if the figures were always in the rock and that Michelangelo merely released them. The sculptures make me think of great footballers like Michael Long and Robert Harvey who seem to have the footballer in them; as if they were always footballers and were meant to be footballers. I wonder what I was meant to be and think it would be a rather severe God who means someone to be a Geelong supporter. I visit museums and art galleries and I think had there been Australian footy in the Renaissance there'd be plenty of sculptures of The High Mark.

In Rome I walk. As I head down from the Forum I get my first glimpse of the Colosseum. It looks just like the MCG when you walk from the city along Brunton Avenue. I go inside and sit on a broken column which has been smoothed on top at about Bay 13. I hear the screams for Gary Ablett. What has changed?

At about the same time I was at the Colosseum, Geelong was running on to Subiaco to play for their lives. I have since seen the tape. We came from behind, got on top, and crushed the Eagles in the last quarter. Ablett, despite wrapping himself around a goalpost, was sensational. We just needed Collingwood to beat Adelaide and we'd be in the finals. I made a call from the Vatican the next day. Collingwood led by five goals early but went down. We had missed out. Bloody Collingwood again. Most of Geelong's disappointments can be traced back to Collingwood. We finished seventh just a game and a half from top spot. This was so Geelong. When a team finishes a game and a half from the top they usually finish second. In a tough year, maybe third. But missing the finals.

Since Geelong was not in the finals I changed my flight. After trekking around Europe for another month I landed back in Brisbane on grand final day. I was very glad I did. I saw Michael Long lead Essendon to a wonderful premiership.

The Dons were lucky though. The flag was rightfully Geelong's.

CHAPTER 15

During the Blight years, everyone talked about what a talented side Geelong was. Everyone knew we had the goods, we just couldn't put it together. Things seemed to be taking a turn for the better when the 1994 finals series commenced. Billy Brownless kicked a goal after the siren against Footscray and we won by five points. Then we had to play the strong Carlton unit at Waverley.

David and Irene and baby Samuel were up on holidays and I went down to the Gold Coast to visit them—and watch the footy. We had high hopes but as the coverage started the mood quickly changed. Bairstow, Couch and Hocking had withdrawn from the match with injury. No chance. There was all this crap about how it would be a great opportunity for some young Cats players. Like who?

David and I settled down to a couple of beers when the TV in the holiday unit went blank. Kaput. It was cactus. We raced to the nearest public venue which turned out to be the Labrador FC where there was a gathering of thirsty footy fans barracking for both sides.

To our surprise, the Cats were sensational. Liam Pickering, Ablett with his six goals, Barnesy. It was one of the great days in the club's history; a day when Geelong broke the spirit of Carlton. It was one of those wins where, that Monday, people go down to the Geringhap Street tattoo shop and get the same tattoo.

That took us into the preliminary final and with a full side back we really took it up to North. We blitzed them in the second quarter kicking seven goals to none—and then we got the staggers. It took Carey and his mob most of the second half to fight back and with a few minutes to go we looked gone. Somehow we got the ball forward and Leigh Tudor popped one into the square from deep in the pocket. He had little control over his kick. It could have gone anywhere but fell to G. Ablett—sheer good fortune. He blasted it through and we had another shot at the flag.

Not too much can be said about the 1994 AFL grand final. We got flogged by the West Coast Eagles, a side which had the originality of a Home Brand label. Absolutely flogged. Humiliated. By eighty points. That was three grand finals in six years. Malcolm Blight could give no more.

I found it very difficult to accept that Gary Ayres, a Hawthorn player who had inflicted considerable pain and suffering on Geelong over the years, would become our coach in 1995. He was reliable, consistent, physically strong, unflappable. How was he going to fit in at Geelong?

In the case of Gary Ayres' first season at Geelong it is difficult to establish cause and effect but somehow we finished second. The bigger surprise was that Brisbane finished eighth in a rather spectacular way.

While the Cats were going well early in the season, the Bears were having a shocker. They had a reasonable list with plenty of young emerging talent—Michael Voss, Jason Akermanis, Justin Leppitsch—but there seemed to be a rift between some of the players and their tough coach, Robert Walls. They'd won four of their first fifteen when I took Beth Gex to the Gabba to see them play.

Beth was in Australia for the world chamber music competition in Melbourne. We sat on the western terrace in the dreamy July sunshine. I raved on about how wonderful a game this was but struggled to find the exact words to describe it. I tried to describe it in terms that she knew. Footy, I explained, is like music. Sometimes there are grand passages of flowing play written for strings. Sometimes it's all brass and crashing cymbals until you come out the other side. Sometimes it's jazz—all improvised and seemingly directionless but somehow the artistry of the performers creates the magic. Sometimes it's even John Paul Young. For Geelong supporters it's usually Leonard Cohen.

I tried to explain it all—thirty years of passion, thirty years of meaning. My voice was enthusiastic but I suspect I made little sense. I kept at it. Footy has colour, movement, strategy. It's fast, spectacular. It's about about overcoming self-doubt. It's about belief. It's about teamwork. It's about committing to a common purpose—and yet players never lose their individuality. It's about risk. It's about truth and beauty. It's magnificent.

What was happening in the middle of the Gabba at that moment was about very few of these things. Hawthorn, one of the bottom sides, was flogging the Bears in a very pedestrian contest. The Bears were trying to bottle things up on the defensive side of the Gabba, and Hawthorn were still getting away. They were eight goals up at three-quarter time when they sought refuge in the shade of the grandstand. Beth Gex laughed when I kept apologising for the poor game.

In the last quarter the Bears kicked a couple of goals and then Stephen Lawrence booted a monster which bounced through and that breathed just a hint of life into the crowd. Another goal and the crowd stirred. Brisbane were starting to believe they were back in it.

The crowd found a bit of voice. Another one and we had what Crackers Keenan calls a 'situation'. The footy was now a proper contest of determined teams. The Bears were irrepressible. It was raining goals. Beth and I were out of our seats with the crowd. The Bears kicked 9.7 to win by seven points and, in one quarter of footy, Beth had seen what my words couldn't describe. Even if this was still only part of the story.

The Bears kept winning. Big wins. They knocked over Adelaide at Footy Park, they beat Sydney in Sydney and they almost rolled Carlton at Princes Park. As the Blues were having one of the most successful seasons of all time this was seen as a measure of the Bears' improvement. They needed to win their last three games, all of which were at home, to keep their finals hopes alive.

Peter and I watched them hammer Richmond and then saw them win a crackerjack game against Essendon under the lights for the first time at the Gabba. The final match of the home and away season, against Melbourne, was booked out before I had a chance to think about getting tickets. That Friday night we were starting to wish we were there so I suggested to Peter that we just go over to the Gabba to see if we could get in.

Peter drops me off at the Stanley Street entrance and I walk over to the security zombie at the turnstile. He tells me the game's sold out. I ask in a voice which is far too loud, 'Mate, what do I need to do to get you to let me in? How about ten bucks?'

He leans forward and says quietly, 'Listen, that's my boss just there.' He nods at him and then whispers conspiratorially, 'Why don't you go around to the Main Street gate.'

I do. The game isn't far from starting. There is no one at the gate except a couple of security zombies. I say to one, 'Mate, will you let me in for twenty bucks?'

He looks at his colleague. 'Hey Bruce, is that an unused ticket I can see in the bin over there?'

'Yeah, it is,' Bruce replies.

The first zombie lets me through and we sneak into the shadows. I tell him I need a second ticket. 'Hey Bruce,' he says, 'is that another unused ticket I can see in the bin?'

'So it is.'

We are in. I just have to pay. I only have a fifty dollar note. When I hand it to him he shakes his head. 'Mate, do you reckon I've got change?' We look at each other. 'This is what we're doing,' he says. 'You go and buy something at that van and get them to put the change on the counter. I'll pick up forty bucks, you take the rest.'

I buy a carton of chips just as Peter arrives at the gate. The chips man puts the cash on the counter. I leave two twenties there. The zombie picks up his dough and we are in. It's a great deal.

The match has just started. We find a spot on the hill but it's so crowded that we can't see the goal square or the goal umpire at our end. Not long after we're there the ball is lobbed into the square to a pack of players obscured from view. Suddenly a body appears above the crowd. It is Sean Smith taking one of the greatest marks of all time. The Bears win another terrific match. They deserve their spot in the eight.

I needed to do some research on my PhD and decided that the month of September was the most suitable to travel to Melbourne to work on my topic. I was becoming increasingly interested in why footy was so popular; why it generated such a following. I looked at my own family. There wasn't a phone call made in the winter months when we didn't talk about Geelong. More often than not these phone calls were made specifically to talk about Geelong.

It intrigued me that we were a Geelong family. My great-grandfather and Papa had both lived in Geelong. Papa was the pastor at Grovedale from 1913 to 1925 and my great-grandparents retired to Geelong at that time. As German Lutheran ministers it surprised me that they had come to love footy as much as they did while in Geelong—Lutherans tended to be suspicious of the world. They tended to remain separate from the broader community—except when it came to footy. Why?

I decided to investigate Geelong and its people to establish the significance of football and of the club. The Geelong Football Club was established in 1859, which makes it one of the oldest football clubs of any code in the world. It has a fascinating history. I would spend September at various libraries and archives in Melbourne and Geelong.

David and a gang of twelve other Adelaide Lutheran types came to Melbourne for the first weekend of the finals. We went to all four games. As I waited to meet them that Friday night I thought again about how different Australian footy crowds are from English soccer crowds. There was a spirit of celebration outside the MCG. Dad and Mum and freckled-faced kids waiting for Uncle Phil and Aunty Marj and their kids. Flags and painted faces and footy jumpers that had been worn every second day for three footy seasons. Kicking the footy using a light post and the bonnet of the cop car for goals. Not realising yet, how much they love the MCG; how the bare trees and the tufty grass and the smell of cooking oil and onion sizzling make them feel at home.

The boys arrive and we sit up the top of the Great Southern Stand. The teams run out. Richmond have a little mascot. He's about two and a half and, as keyed up as people are about the match, the kid steals the show. He runs with the Tigers squad but the footballers get away. They do a whole lap and catch the little tacker who is still sprinting. They run past him so that he disappears in the pack and then appears trailing out the back again. North Melbourne are too strong.

On Saturday afternoon we see Essendon beat West Coast in a dull game at Waverley. The only highlight is the post-match dob—one of the great traditions of AFL footy. I love the morse-code sound of two thousand feet on leather.

We catch the bus and the train to the MCG to see Geelong and Footscray. Geelong have finished second on the ladder yet there is a sense that the game could go either way. Ablett is out. And, after all, it is a contest involving Geelong. David and I have no clue. As Cats supporters we have given up trying to anticipate what will happen. We just hope the Cats play well. They should—that's the problem.

What follows is thirty minutes of bliss. I am with my brother at the MCG, this sacred place where every week the liturgy is chanted, the hymns sung, watching Geelong. The Cats have one of those quarters where *everything* goes right. They are in concert with the gods. The risks they take come off. They are encouraged and their spirits are lifted. They are in a state of grace, as John Carroll calls it. Risks are no longer risks. Difficult manoeuvres are completed automatically. It is magnificent to watch. They move the ball with such pace that Brownless has a paddock to work in. As the umpires wave the flags for another goal you find yourself thinking that you don't deserve it, that it can't continue—yet the footy is sent forward again. This is joy. Billy kicks four in the opening term and the Cats have ten. Ten. True happiness.

The most dangerous thing that Geelong people—players and supporters—can do is think about their happiness. At that instant things change. Geelong people don't believe they have the right to be happy. We feel unworthy. Even when we are in that state of grace we are afflicted with doubt. Our hope is never pure; we are too damaged.

By the time the Geelong players realise what they are doing this night they have fifteen goals on the board. It is only then, when they lead by eighty points near the end of the second quarter, that the fumbling and panicking surface. David spots the change. He looks at me and says, 'It's not over yet.' He is deadly serious.

But this time the ship is righted and we win by fourteen goals. We celebrate. We sing the song over and over:

> We are Geelong the greatest team of all
> We are Geelong we're always on the ball
> We play the game as it should be played
> At home or far away
> Our banners fly on high
> From dawn to dark
> Down at Kardinia Park.

We still haven't had enough footy. We are at the MCG again on Sunday afternoon to watch the Bears frighten Carlton. When they look like getting on top in the third quarter some of the Blues fans, who detect that we are barracking feverishly for the Bears, scream at us: 'I hate turncoat Victorians like you bastards. What's wrong with you?' Apart from a verbal tiff between a North grandma and a Tiger fan on Friday night this is the only instance of ill will we see all weekend. We laugh. Koutoufides goes to full forward and rescues Carlton from a Brisbane side that doesn't know how to win.

Geelong are straight into the preliminary final against Richmond who have won a brutal match against Essendon. Mick and Janelle come to the game. Janelle's father and grandfather played for Richmond. It's cold and wet so we wear those Glad Wrap raincoats. The Cats are in sensational form. Hinkley is a champion. He proves that skill can triumph. The Tigers fans are shattered but halfway through the last quarter they wave their jackets and sing the Tigers song, 'Tigerland', which for a few moments, assumes the stature of 'Abide with Me'.

We win by fifteen goals and are in the grand final— again. Tickets are impossible to find.

During grand final week I spent some time in Geelong where I interviewed Neil Trezise, one of Geelong's great sons. He talked quietly about football and the people of Geelong. I was surprised that he didn't have more to say. It was as if he was talking about something he'd never thought hard about. The importance of the Cats to Geelong was axiomatic.

Nothing really fired him up, either—until we got onto the topic of Gary Ablett. Neil Trezise was an elder statesman of the Geelong community, twenty-eight years their representative in parliament and two-time premiership player for the Cats—and his eyes lit up and he became boyishly excited when he talked about Gary Ablett. We sat for twenty minutes recalling feats of the Great Man. His voice found life. 'I love him,' he said. 'I just love him.'

Neil was a member of the Historical Committee at the club. He asked if I'd like to have a look at the Geelong rooms. We met the next afternoon. It was the Cats' last training of grand final week. We had gone through the gym and were standing in the boot room when Gary Ablett brushed past my shoulder, got a couple of pairs of boots, said a quick hello to Nipper and walked out. He looked strong. This was the bloke who had brought so much joy and happiness to so many people. Including me.

There were a couple of thousand people at the ground. The Cats trained like champions, sweeping the ball from end to end. Crisp handballs were perfectly weighted. Long, spearing passes hit their mark. Goals sailed through at the Hickey Stand end. Surely this was our year? After training a few players stayed out on the track. Buddha was mucking around kicking low, darting fifty-metre torps with his left foot—off one step.

On grand final eve I went to the exhibition of footy art at the Artists' Garden gallery in Fitzroy. It said something about life in Melbourne that artists chose footy as a subject. There were plenty of portraits of Gary Ablett.

Later that night I find myself in the Standard Hotel in Fitzroy. I am still hopeful that I'll find a ticket. Everyone is talking about it being a great grand final. I sit by myself writing a few postcards. I have a couple of pints of Guinness. I feel funny. I start wondering whether I really want Geelong to win the flag.

I try and stop myself having this blasphemous thought but it keeps resurfacing. I have spent a lifetime waiting for Geelong to win the flag. I see the world this way; I know everything from this perspective. The only reality I know is one of hope. Would everything be irrevocably transformed if Geelong won the grand final? Would I be a different person? Would the world be a different place? I am a bit concerned. I jot down a few lines:

Grand Final

Samuel Beckett told me
it was safe to sit in a Fitzroy pub:
no flags there.
So I did.
The golden fire
and the black Guinness
had me thinking of vanquished Richmond
and humming,
'We are Geelong, the greatest team of all.'
But Beckett, disguised as Bizet, cut in
and I thought again:

you can thrash the Tiges,
but Heaven help your whole existence
if you beat the blues.

I have another Guinness to calm myself down.

The next day some people whom I met a few days earlier—Natalie and David—take me to a grand final breakfast at Paul Callery's house. He is a real person and not just a Melbourne rover. Everyone is talking about the Cats' chances again—and how hard it is to get tickets.

We end up watching the game from the East Melbourne Hotel on Hoddle Street about a Doug Wade torp from the MCG. We are the only three in the pub. Geelong bear no resemblance to the team I saw training at Kardinia Park two nights earlier. It's a massacre.

After the game Carlton supporters burst into the pub like the world is theirs—because it is. Geelong supporters are sombre. The universe remains balanced—just as it was meant to be. I talk to people I've never met before: Geelong supporters I feel I've known all my life. I sing the Carlton song over and over with the victors. Sometimes I even start it up again.

Four grand finals in seven years.

I can't live like this. It's too hard. On the plane going back to Brisbane I decide that I'm not going to allow myself to get so caught up in it all.

Never. Never again.

PART 4

We rejoice in our sufferings, knowing that
suffering produces endurance, and endurance produces
character, and character produces hope, and hope does
not disappoint us.

Romans 5:3-5

CHAPTER 16

Things were going to change. I was still going to take an interest in the Cats in 1996, but I had promised not to organise my existence to see every possible Geelong game on TV, hear every possible Geelong moment of radio commentary and read every morsel of printed word about Geelong. By the end of March I knew it was a promise I couldn't keep. Geelong played the very first game of that season. Sitting on the back deck on a balmy Brisbane night, we listened to Ablett kick a bag as the Cats thrashed Melbourne by twenty goals.

It was easier to follow footy in Brisbane by then. We were getting four games on TV each weekend, and there were a lot more radio broadcasts of footy—especially through the ABC's Parliamentary News

Network. Having the footy on the radio was very much part of the rhythm of my existence. In those days Peter 'Smooth' Booth and the peerless Tim Lane did the broadcast on Saturday afternoons and I was able to listen with an unprecedented freedom.

Commentators like Tim Lane call footy as if they love it—because they do. And they call it for an audience who also love footy—and know footy. We know the language of the call. I can picture exactly what is happening when Tim's voice rolls,

'It falls to Knights whose clever handball finds Campbell. Campbell by hand to the running Rogers and the Tigers are away again. One bounce. And another. Surely the Tigers can make something of this. He goes long in the direction of Richardson. But it's *all* Carlton.' You can hear the crowd applauding and Tom Hafey groaning at the back of the box. 'And Hanna mops up for the Blues.'

'All Carlton': we know exactly what Tim Lane means. There's a hint that Rogers' kick wasn't the best option; that the delivery could have been better and that the Blues have read it all easily. And we know that 'mopping up' is just that. The player, despite the threat that has existed, finds himself in a situation where he has time and plenty of team-mates around him. 'Mops up' is almost always followed by description of a successful disposal; in the case of Hanna, something like 'He chips to Bradley in the last line of defence and Carlton are out of trouble again,' at which point Peter Booth would take over.

Over the years the commentators become your companions. They help you to plant marigolds, get rid of weeds, and prune the creeper on the side fence. They are vital to the cleaning of drains and sweeping of verandahs and to the drinking of beer. You never hold them responsible for Geelong losses and you like how they share the victor's joy.

There is an order of service for coverage of the footy: the build-up with interviews and matters of footballing importance, the prediction, and then the game, the post-match, a few minutes of talkback (from supporters in their cars who want to bag the umpires, from farmers at Strathmerton who always thank the boys for their call, and from brave ten-year-olds who want to know whether the panel think Richmond can still make the eight), and finally the broadcast closes with a montage of the game's highlights. Then it's the six o'clock news and you only have to wait a couple of hours before they cross to Adelaide and Roger Wills. As soon as you hear him you know you're at Footy Park, you know that this is football with a South Australian flavour.

I have spent many a Saturday evening listening to the ABC wrap from five until six—the sombre interview from the losers' room and the buoyant interview from the winners'. When Geelong lose I head out the back and water the garden and think. I have spent hours in hose-in-hand contemplation, giving the marigolds far more water than they need. I sometimes wonder whether I'd be a different person if I followed another club.

These days, though, there isn't time to do much after the Saturday afternoon match except head to the Gabba to watch the Lions play. It still seems a little strange to be going to the footy in Brisbane.

The emergence of the national competition has altered footy. It has disrupted what was a meaningful rhythm of football life in Melbourne. That Sullivans world of trams and Gladstone bags and the home and away season, however imagined, is lost. Recently I spent a day going to the old grounds in Melbourne. Each has such individual character—their shape, the scoreboards, the clocks. But they are like old drive-ins. The new footy experience is sanitised, commercialised, standardised.

On the other hand the national competition has allowed more people to see great football. We see so many games on TV now. The whole mindset of TV footy has changed. The footy replays were once about bringing a familiar cultural experience into the lounge rooms of those who valued it. The TV coverage was basic—a couple of cameras and a couple of commentators bringing you what you would have seen had you been at the ground. Now footy is a television product, a 'show' with characters and format so that the principal entity is 'TV footy' rather than footy. I try to see it for what it has always been for me.

There are new elements to the footy week. There is 'Talking Footy' and 'The Footy Show' (which you can watch in Queensland if you're up in the middle of the night). And what did people do at work on Monday mornings before email? These days you spend the first hour checking the results in the office tipping competition, then email some Geelong supporter who's tipped against the Cats when they've managed to get home against Port at Footy Park. Even tipping competitions have altered our footy experience. They mean that you start barracking for favourites rather than underdogs, because that's who you've tipped. You find yourself supporting Carlton against Sydney. This is absurd. You despise everything about Carlton. In the old days South Melbourne beating Carlton by ten goals was nearly as good as a Geelong victory.

Footy is certainly very different on the field these days. Clubs draft athletes rather than footballers. There is less variety of body shape. Clubs also want the full package. They want young kids who can run all day, who can name the capital cities of most South American countries, can call bingo at St Pat's Ladies' Guild meetings, and can appear in the Sunday paper's fashion section. If they can't do all this then it's up to the media department to make it look like they can or to find counsellors who will help them. This now means there is a danger that young blokes who don't fit the stereotype but have the footballer in them may never be drafted.

One of the features of footy is that there has always been a place for all body shapes and sizes and that character has emerged on the field. There's a role for Libber as there's a role for Marcus Ashcroft as there's a role for Justin Madden. But who will sign the Greg Williamses, the Adrian Fletchers, the Serge Silvagnis and Sam Kekoviches?

And what of the system which removes players from their local clubs when they're fifteen and puts them in elite academies and squads? How do these kids learn footy's folklore; the folklore of their local clubs? In the past these talented kids would be the subject of earnest debates over beers in the local on a Thursday night. When was the right time to blood the gifted youngster in the seniors? And what effect does the absence of these talented seventeen-year-olds have on the local leagues?

There have been many changes. Footy, however, remains such a great game that not even those who exploit it for commercial gain have been able to stuff it up. When players run out onto the footy field you don't think about how they were drafted, how much they earn, who sponsors them. Footy is too engaging for that.

When Shane Crawford and Simon Black chase a ball shoulder to shoulder on the wing you think of footy only for what it is at that moment: a grand individual contest within a grander team game.

These days I see more of Brisbane than I do of Geelong. When I go to the Gabba I am keen for

Brisbane to win but really I want to see good footy. The Lions have played some great footy at the Gabba.

Meanwhile Geelong has done it tough. Since the umpires robbed us of a flag in '97 by refusing to pay Leigh Colbert's mark against Adelaide in the semi, we've struggled. We're building a new generation. The old one is gone. Sometimes I wonder whether we'll ever see the likes of them again.

I miss them. We failed together. I miss Billy Brownless. I miss seeing him on the lead, taking the ball on the first bounce, turning on one of those huge arcs the size of that roundabout at Hay and handballing to Mark Bairstow running straight at the goals. I miss Paul Couch and his cheeky smile. I miss him fairy-stepping through the middle while Olympians flash past. Somehow he got the ball and, with that blessed left foot, hit one of the boys on the chest. I miss Kenny Hinkley who was born skinny and never changed and had to rely on the purest of skills. I miss them all.

But it's the Great Man I miss the most. One of the best strokes of fortune in my life is that Gary Ablett played for the Geelong Football Club, because Gary Ablett was a great footballer. He didn't have Bob Skilton greatness, or James Hird greatness. I could see that. I could sense that he had something more; that he played the game eccentrically, uniquely. I wonder what I would have thought of him had he played for Collingwood. Would my eye have focussed on his fear-some physicality, his brutality? Or would it have seen his sheer brilliance? I hope I would have still admired him because he was remarkable.

I miss the thrill of seeing him run onto the ground. I miss the anticipation; the wondering whether he had come to play. Sometimes he didn't—Gary Ablett had his mediocre days. But usually he did, and that's when he consistently did things which left his team-mates gobsmacked. Even on his good days, however, there was a feeling he could have done more. Perhaps we empathise with him because he never lived up to his potential. Perhaps he feared it.

Perhaps we relate to him because some of his finest performances were in losing sides. Apart from the '89 grand final, he kicked fourteen one day and we still lost to Essendon. He kicked ten when we went down to Adelaide at Footy Park. I was there that night. There was an acknowledgment—even from Crows supporters—that there was something about him.

I miss his athleticism, his pace, his power: this balding man, with round shoulders and a big backside. This man who would appear above the pack. Often. A man who could explode. And yet he played with such a dispassionate expression. He was rarely jubilant and I can't remember him ever showing frustration at his team-mates.

He could also implode. He didn't have Polly Farmer's serenity. Farmer once said, 'I'm just trying to understand that ball.' His search for truth extended outwards. Perhaps Gary Ablett was trying to understand himself. Perhaps it is his turmoil and tragedy which draws us to him. We don't know enough of him. I miss his mystery and complexity.

I am not ashamed to say that, for all these reasons, Gary Ablett was my hero. That he merely drifted away makes his absence even sadder. I wish he were still playing. More than anything, though, I miss how he made me feel like a little boy again; he made me feel like tugging on my father's sleeve and saying, 'Did you see that, Dad?'

He made me smile: that smile that comes from further within you than you can imagine or understand, but makes you feel that somehow, though the world remains the same, all is not vanity.

As you get older and footy continues to occupy much of your waking time you think more and more about why. You read things which help you make sense of the world and realise that often the ideas relate to footy as well. I stumbled across Paul Tillich and Victor Frankl, who wrote about things far more important than football, and could see what they were on about. They confirmed my view that people have a desire 'to be' and a will to meaning. We choose life and in living we crave things which are meaningful. We tire of things which just fill in time; the hollow; the meaningless.

People don't tire of footy. It matters to them. It's part of them. There's something in footy; something more. It is the same something which you might find in a powerful novel or a piece of music or a great film.

Footy is poetry. When you read a poem you sense that the words have had some effect on you—emotional, spiritual, intellectual. You feel it. It is very hard to find the words which describe that poetic effect. It is the poetry rather than the analysis of the poetry which matters. The poem is the shared experience. So it is with footy. It is a language itself. Yet we want more. We are still drawn into the search for the words which help explain why it is so meaningful.

For two AFL seasons I had a regular Monday sports column in the *Australian*. I had written a few pieces about footy for the 'Observer' section and, as a result, a risk-taking editor drafted me into the side. I tried to find some of those elusive words to describe an element of footy, to remind people of how they may have felt watching the footy, and to invite them to speculate. There was always much to write about. There is so much in a quarter of footy, a game of footy, a weekend of footy, a lifetime of footy. But how do you find the right words? How do you describe Andrew McLeod's third quarter in the 1998 AFL grand final? How do you describe such creativity? How do you tell people that he made you believe in perfection?

Footy is about these things. It confirms your suspicion that there is something more. It alerts you to the existence of the soul. It invites you to be faithful. It *demands* you be faithful, and loyal. And just when you are doubting it you see a game which makes you realise why you are so enthusiastic about it. You see courage, commitment, personal sacrifice, skill and beauty, and you are uplifted. Footy is one of the few places in contemporary life where you experience the transcendent.

Footy is also about suffering and suffering can be uplifting. Suffering is the natural state—especially for Geelong supporters. It is honest. And how we respond to that suffering is elemental. Suffering can bring us together and it is only when we understand the suffering of others that we understand the fullness of joy. So when we watch the premiership flag unfurled there are tears. In those tears there is at once joy and suffering.

The poet Virgil was no dill. He had never heard of footy or the Geelong Football Club yet he observed *'Sunt lacramae rerum et mentem mortalia tangunt.'* 'There are tears at the centre of things and mortality touches the heart.' Footy is about life in the face of death; hope in the face of despair. Footy is about the things at the very centre of existence, like religion is.

I am in Melbourne again. Round twenty-one, 2001. It is Buddha Hocking's last game at Kardinia Park. Geelong are to play the Brisbane Lions. On a drizzly Sunday, Martin Flanagan picks me up. He is writing a piece on Buddha for the *Age*.

We head through Collingwood, past Victoria Park,

into Smith Street. Around the cemetery. Along Racecourse Road. Past the Western Oval, a footy ground that means a lot to Martin. Down the Geelong Road. We talk about all sorts of things. We talk about footy, Geelong and Garry Hocking. We talk about family and understanding where you come from; about acknowledging the depth of those connections and knowing that those closest to you are growing older. That you are growing older yourself.

Martin Flanagan understands time. Because he does, he asks you questions other people wouldn't. He gets straight to the things which matter. And he tells you things. He wants to know you and he wants you to know him. His conversation makes you realise how deeply he empathises with people. He lives their sadness. He also delights in those things that sustain us all—like hearing stories and telling stories, like going to the footy, like following a footy team.

We meet John Dunne and make our way into Kardinia Park. This will be only the third game I've seen at this ground. The Cats have had a disappointing season. The experts had suggested we'd be one of the improvers in 2001. In truth we've gone backwards.

The club knows it is a significant day. Many past champions have been invited and they stand in a long line on the ground in front of the members' stand. They have so many stories. The people in the crowd tell their stories of watching them play. It is a nostalgic day.

In Australian English we have a thin understanding

of the word 'nostalgia'. It tends to be used to describe a lament for the past—that somehow life was great then and that things would be much better if we just went back there. In the Latin languages, words like *nostalgie* in French and Spanish and *saudade* in Portuguese are far more complex; richer. Their nostalgia is the idea of returning home, home to the things which have formed you.

I am not defined by my love of the Geelong Football Club but footy is one of those things that takes me home. It reminds me of my very self; my real self; my true self. Footy—the heroic players, the loyal and enthusiastic fans, the spectacular action that is a game of footy—makes me feel that life has meaning. Footy is not the most important thing in the world but it alerts me to the things which are.

The group of past Geelong champions stand together on their home ground. They look old. We see their grey hair and their shrinking bodies. They greet each other like men who once did something important together—retired pastors, or returned soldiers. They chat and laugh. They exude a mutual respect. There is a mood of thankfulness, that they have been privileged to be part of the Geelong Football Club. Gary Ablett is not among them.

They watch as Buddha comes out, and they remember. They remember when they first played, when they retired. But it is Buddha's day and they remember his gallant career. Buddha's wife Melina and their three little children are with him. They walk through the banner together. The crowd watch intently.

People love Buddha. They love his boyishness, the sense that he'd be able to think up an excuse for not doing his tech drawing homework (like we would). They love his rock-like body. They even love his haircut—because that's Buddha. They have watched him under packs, as hard a player as has ever played at Geelong. They have celebrated with him and they have forgiven him. They have seen his determination and his skill, how he can use a footy, how he understands the game. They also know that his body will no longer permit him to do what he wants to do. People think of themselves. There are tears in the outer: tears of happiness and sadness; tears of remembering; tears of life.

The Cats take up their positions and there is such emotion, enthusiasm and determination that we dominate the first quarter. The game is urgent, disjointed. Out of the mess, Buddha kicks a goal. People rise from their seats. In the outer, middle-aged blokes with Countdown hair punch the air; scarved receptionists screech; farmboys spill their beers; kids wave their flags. We can win this.

The Lions hardly go forward. But we squander our chances. Our disposal is terrible. We don't have the skills. The Lions work their way into the contest. During the second quarter they impose their will on the chaos, transforming the staccato scrap into an open, flowing game. Suddenly there are loose men everywhere. We watch a majestic football side use the footy with scintillating skill, and we lose. I have never seen Geelong win at Kardinia Park.

Buddha does a slow lap, walking along the fence with one of his kids in his arms. He greets the people as they lean across. Many he knows. Many he doesn't. Some, like Toby Bairstow, he has played with. They embrace across the advertising. What memories there are in the meeting of their eyes. What fraternity.

Martin writes his article. It appears on the front page. Buddha was a champion. We'll tell our kids about him.

They'll know their own.

Acknowledgments

It takes a lot of support to follow a footy team like Geelong—and to write about it.

Thanks to Dad and Mum and my three brothers, Peter, David and Michael, for helping me to remember and for reading and commenting on the early chapters. Thanks to Eric Mounsey and Anthony W. Collins for their sporting generosity. Thanks to Tim Stollznow, Bayden Findlay, Gideon Haigh, Martin Flanagan, John Dunne, Ade (the banker), Ben Dobson and Rick Mitchell for their assistance and support.

Thanks to Mike Selleck for reading and commenting—and, especially, listening.

Thanks to Bayden and Cale (the milliner) for spending days visiting milk bars in the hope that we could unlock the secret of that milk bar smell—and find the words to describe it.

Thanks also to Simon George, Steve Clarke and the Lord Stanley Hotel (the only place to go for a steak before the footy).

Thanks to Patty Brown, and also to Melanie Ostell and Mandy Brett and the people of Text Publishing.

Thanks to Susan. I'm sorry that you've become part of the Geelong tragedy but your loyalty has warmed my heart.

And finally, thankyou to all those who have ever strapped on a boot for the Geelong Football Club.